The Author:
Les Woodson is a minister, writer, and evangelist of the United Methodist Church. Born in Louisville, Kentucky, he attended Asbury College, after which he earned degrees from the University of Louisville, Scarritt College, and Southern Baptist Theological Seminary. He also has a D.D. from American Divinity School.

Since 1970, Woodson has authored eight books, including *What You Believe and Why* and *Evangelism for Today's Church* (Zondervan), and *Hell and Salvation* and *Population, Pollution, and Prophecy* (Revell).

Les Woodson's hobby is wood-working. He specializes in building Early American cherry reproduction furniture, and together with his sons built his own Early American barn-house. Married to the former Betty Eastridge, Woodson is the father of two daughters and five sons.

The Beginning

A Study of Genesis

Les Woodson

While this book is designed for the reader's personal use and profit, it is also intended for group study. A leader's guide is available from your local bookstore or from the publisher at 95¢.

Published by

VICTOR BOOKS

a division of SP Publications, Inc.
WHEATON, ILLINOIS 60187

Scripture quotations are from the King James Version unless otherwise identified. Other versions quoted include the *New American Standard Bible* (NASB), © 1971 by The Lockman Foundation, La Habra, Calif.; the *Amplified Bible* (AMP), © 1965 by Zondervan Publishing House, Grand Rapids, Mich.; and *The Living Bible* (LB), © 1971, Tyndale House Publishers, Wheaton, Ill. All quotations used by permission.

Library of Congress Catalog Card Number: 74-79161
ISBN: 0-88207-713-9

VICTOR BOOKS
A division of SP Publications, Inc.
P.O. Box 1825 • Wheaton, Ill. 60187

CONTENTS

INTRODUCTION

There's no place to begin like the beginning. And that's what you're doing when you study the Book of Genesis.

The word *genesis* is a transliteration into English of the Greek word for *beginning*. You can see the word *genesis* reflected in terms in common use. Our verb *generate* comes from the same root and means "to get something going." When we speak of *generations* we are talking about successive stages or epochs of beginning. The word *generations* appears 10 times in the Book of Genesis, and some biblical students think it provides a natural outline of the contents.

The opening word of the Hebrew Old Testament means "in the beginning," and it's from this prepositional phrase that the title is derived. When the Old Testament was translated into Greek during the third century before Christ (the Septuagint translation), this book of beginnings was given the title "Genesis."

While Genesis is complete in itself and can be studied independently, it must also be seen as a part of a much larger work. The first five books of the Old Testament form what is called "The Pentateuch" (meaning "five books"). Genesis deals with creation, Exodus with the enslavement and deliverance of the Hebrews in Egypt, Leviticus with the priestly class and its ethical and moral codes, Numbers with travels and census-taking in the newly-formed nation, and Deuteronomy with a restatement of the old laws for a new generation. In an even larger context, the Book of Genesis must be seen in its relation to the unfolding drama of the kingdom of God and the redemption of man. This means that it cannot be divorced from any part of the Old or New Testaments. What God began in Genesis, He will finish in the manner described in Revelation. And every writing between these two books is significant in God's plan for His world.

Traditionally, the entire Pentateuch is credited to Moses, the man who delivered the Hebrews from Egypt and was the first lawgiver in the emerging nation of Israel. Genesis nowhere tells us its

7

author. The ancient Jewish community attached the title: *The First Book of Moses*. References to the "Law of Moses" are found in 2 Chronicles 23:18 and 30:16, and the "Book of Moses" is mentioned in 35:12. But no such reference is found in Genesis itself.*

Destructive higher critics have gone to great lengths to prove that Moses did not write the book. But the critics do not agree among themselves any more than they agree with the traditionalists who hold to belief in Mosaic authorship.

The so-called JEP theory is the critics' explanation of how Genesis came to be. This theory argues that at least three written documents can be discerned in the 50 chapters of Genesis. These three documents tell essentially the same ancient story, though there are differences and even some contradictions. The documents have been ingeniously interwoven by the hands of succeeding redactors to form one continuous narrative.

The J document is supposed to be the work of a prophet from the southern kingdom (Judah) who uses the name *Jahweh* (Yahweh) for God. The E writer was from the northern kingdom (Ephraim) and was a prophet who used the more general *Elohim* for God. The P document is said to be a much later editing of the creation story by priests (P for priest) about 500 years before Christ. The dates given for J and E are the ninth and eighth centuries before Christ, respectively.

The whole documentary system of JEP becomes so complex that you can't see the forest for the trees. Scholars get into involved debates over very minute details of documentation. This is not to discredit scholarship. We owe a sizeable debt to biblical scholars who have reverently brought illumination on difficult problems of Bible study. But it's possible to become so preoccupied with the structure of a book that we miss the heart and core of its message. And it's possible to create so much complexity around a segment of scriptural study that all but the intellectual giants are driven away from Bible study altogether.

---

* The New Testament makes it clear that Jesus believed in the Mosaic authorship of the Pentateuch. Jesus said to the Jews, "For had ye believed Moses, ye would have believed Me: for he wrote of Me. But if ye believe not his writings, how shall ye believe My words?" (John 5:46-47) Notice that Jesus refers specifically to Moses' "writings"— not just the giving of the 10 Commandments, but the whole of the written record we know as the Pentateuch. The Jews who heard Him knew exactly which books Jesus was talking about. There are other New Testament references to Mosaic authorship: Matthew 8:4; 19:7; Mark 12:19, 26; Luke 24:27, 44. If we accept the testimony of Jesus Christ and the Gospel writers, we cannot seriously question the Mosaic authorship of the Pentateuch.

Little objection can be raised to the existence of ancient creation stories prior to the time of Moses. No doubt numerous oral traditions were handed down from mouth to ear by early peoples. Creation stories similar to the one in the Bible have been discovered in writings of primitive cultures outside the Hebrew tradition. The existence of such creation stories only substantiates the view that all of them found their origin in a common source. That source may have been Adam himself, who told the original story to Seth; hence it was told to men like Enoch, Methuselah, Noah, Shem, and Abraham.

In light of the apostasy of ancient men, which destroyed even their bond of language (Genesis 11:1-9), it is not difficult to see how the creation story may have become corrupted. As men developed a polytheistic religious system, the account of the world's origin took on varying hues of legend. The confusion of tongues at Babel would, understandably, have led to a morass of perverted attempts at explaining the universe and man himself.

Thus when time came for the establishment of a nation of people through whom man's Redeemer would come, God moved to clear up the whole subject of origins. Therefore, an accurate account of universal creation by one God was entrusted to the one man capable of receiving and preserving it at that moment in history—Moses.

For anyone who reverences the Scriptures as the Word of God, there is every reason to believe that Moses was given a direct revelation from God as to how the world began. Indeed, either God revealed the details of creation to someone—since no one was there when it happened, or else man made up the whole thing. Divine revelation is an absolute necessity if we are to have any authentic information.

The Book of Genesis reveals the past even as the Book of Revelation reveals the future. Wouldn't we expect that the God who reveals the future through inspired prophecy would also reveal the past through inspired history? The presupposition on which this book is based is that the Genesis account is pure history and tells in a remarkably clear manner the way the universe began and the way in which God communicated with His creation.

Genesis is primarily a book about God. Nowhere does it attempt to prove the existence of this divine Creator. His existence is taken for granted—His being is assumed as needing no proof. It remained for passing centuries to cultivate the kind of sophistication which induced atheism. Man was originally a believer in one God, later in many gods, and eventually some of his offspring decided that there is no god at all (see Romans 1:20-28). But it was only as he rationalized himself into disbelief that man was able to disown his awareness of the divine. The passage of time dulled man's sensitivity to the Creator. In the infancy of creation, the touch of God upon His world was too fresh to deny His existence. A nontheistic theory was not even thinkable.

The first book of the Bible is about man as well as God. To be more exact, it is an epic about six men. Hundreds of people appear on the stage of human history in the Genesis narrative, but most of them have only walk-on parts. A few are given some lines, but it is obvious that they are not key figures. The leading parts are played by Adam, Noah, Abraham, Isaac, Jacob, and Joseph. Each man was molded and fashioned by the God of creation into the kind of person needed to further the eternal plan of Jehovah for the world, for from the beginning God had designed a kingdom of mutual love and communication through which He could reign over all of creation in righteousness.

Running throughout the entire Bible is a central theme: *the kingdom of God.* It begins with Abraham. The struggles of men and women living through the birth pangs of a divine kingdom on earth is as exciting a drama as could be portrayed by all the modern media with their lavish props. No one could begin to imagine such a plot. All eternity is engaged in bringing it to pass.

Some 4,000 years have come and gone since the opening curtain was raised, and the grand and concluding act, when the Messiah shall return to perfect the reign of God upon the earth, is still future. But the stage is being set for that event, and the curtain call may be only moments away. What was begun in Genesis, continued in the Gospels, and pursued until the present day, will find its culmination in the return of the King of kings, as depicted in the Apocalypse. The Davidic kingdom will be restored to Israel in the land promised to them in Genesis. And the Messiah Himself will sit on that ancient throne.

None of the writings of Scripture is more foundational than Genesis. As the foundation stone, it is placed where it naturally belongs—at the beginning of the written revelation of God.

For too many people the Bible is a collection of literature—some parts more interesting than others—but without any predesigned pattern by which one section is related to another. It is like having 66 building blocks, each shaped different from the other, with no blueprint for putting them together. Or, to change the analogy a bit, the Bible is like a jigsaw puzzle which appears to have few if any interlocking pieces. No matter how it is put together, it doesn't seem to create the correct design. In fact, in forcing the biblical books to create the kind of picture thought to be religiously necessary, we often have pieces left over and large gaps in the puzzle. But rather than admit that we have an inaccurate design on our hands, we use ingeniously devised methods to prove that the sections of the Bible which are left out are unimportant and that the holes are of no particular consequence.

But once the key is discovered the entire collection fits together in such a unique way that the loss of one single section would destroy the intended effect. The key is the little nation of *Israel,* which God called into being through the person of Abraham. The origins of that nation are described in Genesis. And the rest of the Bible is a revelation of God's dealings with man in an unchanging plan to realize His eternal kingdom in which Israel plays such a crucial role. Thus, what we see in this book is basic to our study of the whole Bible.

The following exposition of the biblical book of beginnings is not meant to deal with every meticulous detail of exegesis. Where the meaning of a passage hinges on a word, we will take time to examine the words carefully. Otherwise, our study is geared to give a simple, practical understanding of Genesis. The work is not heavily documented, though much research has gone into its production. It is written out of the study and experience of a long pastoral ministry.

Genesis is a great book with a tremendously important story to tell.

Let's begin . . .

1
THE CREATION
OF THE UNIVERSE

Genesis 1:1—2:25

No one knows how old the universe is. Neither the biblical scholar nor the secular scientist can speak with any final authority. Using fragmentary dating information found in the Old Testament (the ages of the patriarchs and the reigns of kings), Archbishop Ussher arrived at the late date of 4004 B.C. for the creation of man.

But there was a basic flaw in the archbishop's approach. In some instances the genealogies omit whole generations. It is possible that vast periods of time may have been ignored because of the ancients' natural concern with the most important figures in their history. We have no way of knowing how many less notable personalities (and there would have been far more of these than there were VIPs) are not mentioned in the genealogies. But they would add considerably to the numbering of the years.

Another difficulty in dating creation arises from the insurmountable task of determining the length of time which lapsed from the dawn of creation to the creation of Adam on the sixth day. Though some insist that the days of creation were 24-hour days, many earnest Bible students believe that the days of creation represent vast stretches of time. The psalmist affirmed that "a thousand years in Thy sight are but as yesterday" (Ps. 90:4). Peter amplified that idea by saying, "Do not let this one fact escape your notice, beloved, that with the Lord one day is as a thousand years, and a thousand years as one day" (2 Peter 3:8, NASB). The Creator exists in eternity, where time has no meaning. Segments of time as we know it (seconds, minutes, hours, weeks, months, years, centuries) are devices by which man keeps track of past, present, and future. With God there is only the progressive present—no past or future—just the continuous "I Am" (Ex. 3:14).

The eternity of God is a concept so far-reaching that we find ourselves in a fog when confronted with the bare thought. To say that God is eternal is to say that He had no beginning and will have no end. If man cannot comprehend with ease the limitless reaches of space, how do we expect him to conceive of the time-lessness of eternity? Both space and time stretch the human mind to its maximum elasticity. Though to our minds everything should have a stopping place, space itself does not. And though time itself should have a point of termination, eternity does not. The mind of man is so programmed to the beginning and ending of material things that it is baffled and "does not compute" when thrust into the midst of either infinity or eternity.

Spokesmen for natural science say that man has been on earth for at least two million years. They push the beginning of the universe back even farther into the dim past. So Ussher and these natural scientists are obviously in conflict, and the debate about the earth's age goes on. But it is possible that the "moment of beginning" is not to be thought of in terms of time at all. The date of the divine act of creation may elude our methods of calculation precisely because it is not to be construed as a point in time. Could it not rather be that creation should be thought of as a divine act in the timelessness of eternity?

If this is true, then both the Ussher camp and the dedicated men of science may be wasting their efforts in attempting to pinpoint the precise time of creation. But one thing we do know, that "whenever" the universe began to be, God was there and He did it! The opening words of Genesis, "In the beginning God," clearly communicate the eternity of the Creator and possibly the timeless-ness of His eternal creation

How It All Began (1:1—2:3).
Prelude to the first day (1:1-2)

"Created" comes from the Hebrew word transliterated into English as *bara*. Of the three words used in the creation story to describe the act of creating, this is the most illuminating for our study. *Bara* is used exclusively of the activity of God. While the idea of creation *ex nihilo* (out of nothing) is not required by the term itself, it is clear that the writer intends us to understand that to be the case in this opening verse.

The context determines whether the creation of any particular subsequent part of the new cosmos is made from nothing or is fashioned and molded by God from material already created. The significant fact is that when *bara* is used it always indicates a *distinct action* of the Creator. This excludes the natural processes of evolution from one state or level of life to another. In each instance, God is engaged in the act of making something brand new and so uniquely different from all that went before it as to require His *special* attention.

Initially, whether at a point in time or as a timeless event of eternity, the appearance of some semblance of mixed solids and gases was needed as a raw substance on which to work. One of the interesting observations quickly made by the discerning student of the creation account is that God did not complete His creation the same "moment" in which He commenced it. That is, God developed the new, crude cosmos in stages. (Similarly, in the New Testament, Jesus employed two stages of healing in returning sight to a blind man's eyes—Mark 8:22-26.) Why God did not make the universe all at once we do not know. It is clearly stated that it was created in stages, each dependent upon those preceding it.

What we see coming from the will of the Creator at first is an "earth (the revelation to man concerned only that part of creation which was to be his native habitat) without form and void" (v. 2). A hot, seething, mass of solidifying energy might be a fairly accurate description of what we would have witnessed had we been present. From a distance, the earth might have looked like a fog-shrouded, whirling ball of boiling water. With no atmosphere (that was not yet created), there was darkness everywhere, an absence of light accented by the steaming haze which rose from the spinning mass. Internal heat, rising to meet the waters which completely covered the earth, would have created a gigantic, steaming display of energy.

Our concept of the Eternal Spirit who "created the heavens and the earth" is that of power and love. If He is all-powerful, then His mind or will may be said to exert dynamic energy. This would mean that creation was an act of the divine will, that God had only to say the word and that which was desired came to be. Modern science is aware that as matter can be converted into energy, so energy can be converted into matter.

On that first morning of creation, the explosive fireworks which sparkled and spewed across the void were only the side effects of the burst of divine energy which was converted into masses of discernible and tangible matter. It is quite normal to think in terms of God's having created the universe like a man would make a clay ball. But if there were nothing with which to begin except God Himself, then the picture must be changed completely. The Creator must be visualized as *willing* the cosmos into existence, causing it to be by the sheer force of the divine mind.

The first day (1:3-5)

The creation of light is characteristic of the nature and being of God. We would expect to find the mark of the Creator upon His creation. "The heavens are telling the glory of God; and the firmament shows and proclaims His handiwork" (Ps. 19:1, AMP). The brightness of the starry hosts, the grandeur of the sun and moon, the luminous expanse of the heavens awed the ancients. The revelation of God in nature is everywhere about us, but light is especially characteristic of Him.

John rejoices in divine light: "The light shines in the darkness, and the darkness did not overcome it" (John 1:5, NASB). And in his first epistle, he writes, "This is the message we have heard from Him and announce to you, that God is light, and in Him there is no darkness at all" (1 John 1:5, NASB). The creation of light was, in a very real sense, the coming of a transcendent God into that which He had made. At this juncture, the Spirit which had moved over the face of the darkened waters entered into an immanent relationship with His creation.

Though the sun, moon, stars, and planets do not appear in the order of events recorded until the fourth day, it seems that the creation of the sun, at least, took place during this first day. Because of the heavy gases and the impenetrable haze, the source of light was unseen. Only the luminous glow emitted by the sun's rays was viewable. Everything remained in an indistinct form with shaded outlines that gave an eerie appearance to a waking universe.

During the first period of creation, however, the presence of light was discernible enough that its cyclic absence was conspicuous. Thus, God called the interval of darkness by a name rendered *night*. He also gave a name to the interval when the light was obvious— *day*. The separation of the two was effected on the very first day.

With man there is a clearly defined difference between what he says and what he does. His activity may *result* from what he says (in the sense of instructive thought processes) and may *coincide* with the thought or speech as well. But the two are not the same. Man may think, speak, or will without acting, and it is probably true that he can act without thinking.

With God the procedure seems to be different. What He does and what He says are one and the same. When the Creator says, "Let there be light," He also makes light. The will of God is synonymous with the act of God. What He wills, He does; and He does nothing without willing it. God did not want light and then create it. As He wanted it, His will became reality.

As the first day ends, the author refers to it as beginning in the evening, which is followed by the morning. The ancient man's day began at sundown and ended at the same hour the next day. For God to move from darkness to light symbolically suggests that the divine progression is always an improvement. He never works toward the night, but inevitably moves toward the new day in the world which He has made.

The second day (1:6-8)

It is unfortunate that the word *firmament* is used in the King James and some other English translations to describe that which was called forth from the chaos at the dawn of the second day. *Firmament* suggests something hard and *firm* and probably reflects the view of early translators that the starry heaven is like an inverted bowl, the rim of which rides upon the mountainous edge of the earth. Before the translation of the Hebrew Old Testament into the Septuagint (Greek version) in the third century before Christ, the word was understood in its original meaning, not as something firm at all, but rather as a vast, expansive area.

When it is recognized just what this *firmament,* or better, *expanse,* was intended to do, there is no further confusion as to precisely what it was that God made on the morning of this second day. It was the atmosphere. (Apparently, there was no more atmosphere during the first period of creation than that which exists in outer space. If the earth were to be habitable, the sphere in which life would exist would have to be made conducive.) The purpose of the *firmament,* or atmosphere, was to dispel the disorderly water which everywhere covered the earth and saturated the area outside it.

The mist and steam which emanated from the boiling water on the surface of the new earth was thick enough to make the distinction between earth water and heavenly water impossible. Since God's plan was to make three kinds of living things (fowl, fish, and animal) it was necessary that orderly habitats be brought from the confusion which was neither atmosphere nor land, but only unimaginable wetness.

Once the firmament had come to be, the waters began to seek their proper levels—that which would be useful on earth and that which would be needed in the cloudy heavens, although these upper waters may have been far higher than the ordinary cloud formations which today produce rain.* The division did not exclude the obvious interchange of water between the heavens and the earth, but rather made such interchange possible. As long as there was no division, there could be no transference back and forth such as we have in the rain which was later to be provided.

Separating the two bodies of water (earthly and atmospheric) created an open area in between, which would gradually dry and clear so that by the fourth day the sun itself would be visible. Thus God made the atmosphere and gave it the name *heaven*.

The third day (1:9-13)

The next phase in bringing order out of the chaos was to restrict the waters upon the earth to prescribed areas. With meticulous care the Lord began the drying process which would form the land. As the new earth began to cool, the solid mass beneath the water buckled and pushed its way upward into the atmosphere. The high spots formed continents with variations in levels to develop into a picturesque land of jagged mountains and deep valleys as accents for the plains.

As the dry land pushed up through the waters (the account uses the word "appear"), the rolling waves sought the lower areas and thus were imprisoned forever in their places which the Creator named *seas*. On this third day the Lord brought forth final order out of the original formless void and made the new world fit for plants and creatures soon to move upon the land, in the waters, and through the atmosphere.

That which God had made—the light, atmosphere, water, and

---

* Robert P. Benedict has an interesting explanation of the firmament from a scientific viewpoint in *Journey Away from God* (Old Tappan, N.J., Fleming H. Revell Co., 1972), pp. 48-51.

land (called sun, heavens, seas, and earth)—was surveyed by its author and declared "good" (v. 10). Before man's sin, the universe was as God wanted it. There was not a trace of flaw in anything which was made. A veritable paradise awaited God's creatures. The Lord was pleased with His works. He would later place a dominant creature within the midst of the world to preserve the excellence which characterized its beginning and to have a special relationship to Him.

As yet there was no rain (Gen. 2:5-6). Only an extremely high humidity lingered in the remaining heat to produce a tropical climate ideal for the growth of vegetation. Inherent within the earth, air, and water were the qualities required for generating and perpetuating a multitudinous assortment of living greenery.

Willing the appearance of vegetation, the Creator watched with great satisfaction the emergence and rapid growth of every conceivable kind of plant life. Within everything that grew there was seed to reproduce in kind for the duration of the earth's life. The rate of growth was so accelerated by the ideal situation that the entire world was soon covered with a carpet of living green.

The fourth day (1:14-19)

Some find a science-religion conflict in the stated presence of light on the initial day of creation before the appearance of the sun, moon, and stars on the fourth day. It is true that there can ordinarily be no natural light without the sun. Even the moon is only reflective of the sun's rays. But there need be no contradiction here between the findings of science and the biblical account.

Numerous explanations have been offered by scholars who respect both the ancient account and modern observations. The simplest, and probably the most likely possibility, is that the source of light (that is, the sun) was created on the first day and coincided with the statement, "and there was light." Only as the thick, gaseous haze and watery mists cleared away from the atmosphere did the distinct and separate body of the sun become clear.* Naturally, such density in the space between the earth and the celestial bodies would have obscured the lesser light of the moon and stars.

The sun, moon, and stars were to "be for signs and for seasons and for days and years" (v. 14). Though God dwells in timeless-

---

* Of note is the use of two different Hebrew words. For "light" in the account of the first day, the word used is 'or (the existence of light as a phenomenon). In the reference found in the account of the fourth day the word is me'orot (sources of the light phenomenon).

ness, His creatures are subject to both time and space. Therefore, the regularity of the appearance and disappearance of the heavenly lights was to make it possible for man to divide time into usable segments. Our calendar is structured on the dependability of the celestial lights. There could be no seasons before this stage of creation. The tropical climate created by the internal heat of the new earth and the high humidity was without change. As the earth cooled and became dependent for its warmth on an outside force, the tropical climate fluctuated and seasons developed.*

The fifth day (1:20-23)
Having set the bounds for the seas and cleared the atmosphere of its mists, the Creator was now prepared to populate both sea and air with living creatures. The entire work of the first three days was done for the purpose of making the universe habitable for a variety of animate beings. The great pools of water were now to be stocked with every conceivable kind of marine creature. Each was made with all the needed biological faculties to enable it to thrive in a watery environment. The fowl of the air were localized in the atmosphere and acclimated to the open air.

At this juncture in the creation story, the word *bara* (created, v. 21) is used the second time. The origin of animal life was the result of a distinct act of God by which He created something totally new and unrelated to anything yet made. The creation of animal life was abruptly new, as was the creation of the universe on the first day. The biblical account does not suggest an evolutionary hypothesis which affirms that each higher form of life evolved from some lower type of existence. Animal life did not spring from plant life. It was created (*bara*) entirely new and independent of what had gone before.

When the Scriptures repetitiously affirm after the appearance of each new form of life, "according to its kind," this is an emphatic statement that God did not mix the basic levels of organic life. Plant life produced more plants, not animals. And animals reproduced in kind. Birds did not produce fish, and sea monsters did not give birth to birds. Everything which had been made was designed for orderliness, not confusion. As there had been a separation between the heavens and the earth, the sea and the land, so

---

* Some students believe the seasons were not established until after the Flood, and that, in fact, the tilting of the earth on its axis caused both the flood and our present pattern of seasons (Gen. 8:22).

now there would be a clear-cut separation between plant life and animal existence. Each level of life was created by God as He desired it to be, without ambiguity as to which category it may have been a part of or which kind of life it was designed to produce.

The sixth day (1:24-31)

The forms of animal life destined to dwell upon the land rather than in the water or air were created on the sixth day. Each act of the Lord resulted in a higher form of life than that which preceded it. A multitude of animal sub-species inhabits the earth today. Some of them are the result of cross-breeding manipulated by man, but in the beginning each *species* was created exactly as God willed, complete and perfect. Three categories of land animals are mentioned: "cattle and creeping things and beasts of the earth." In each instance, the species were not to mix but to reproduce "according to their kinds." It was not in the plan of the Master Designer that a cow would breed with a tiger or a cat with an armadillo.

While man has developed numerous variations in each divinely-created species, he has not made a single new species since the sixth day of creation. We use the term *species* here in the sense of a natural interbreeding family whose offspring continue the reproductive design. A tiger, cougar, and leopard may interbreed, for example, because they are not three distinct species, but only one. But none of them is successful in breeding with a dog or a jackal and creating a new species which can reproduce.

Reserved for His last act of creation was God's masterpiece—man. Destined to be custodian of the earth and lord of all other living things, man was to be the crowning glory of God's creative activity. For this reason, God lavished all His care upon the creature who was to be most like Himself.

If man were to "have dominion" over everything which had been made, then he would have to be similar to the One who created all. He would need to reflect the divine nature and understand the divine plan for the world. The Hebrew word *bara* is again used (v. 27) to express a distinct act of God by which He created a form of life totally different and distinct from anything earlier made. Just as animal life did not evolve from plant life, so man did not evolve from the lower level of animal existence. The custodian of the universe was to be human, neither divine nor like the previously created animals. There would be no mixing of the

THE CREATION OF THE UNIVERSE / 21

species which would result in some form of *humanimal*—less than man but more than beast. Nor was there to be a progression from beast to man. Man was made, as the animals had been, complete and perfect.

The image of God

To speak of making man in the *likeness* and *image* of God demands some clarification. To be made in the image of God means to be *like* the Creator Himself. But in what way? It hardly needs be mentioned that the physical appearance and biological character-istics of the human species have nothing to do with the divine likeness. "God is spirit" (John 4:24, NASB), without body or visible form. The Eternal Spirit had no thought of man's *looking* like God. Kinship with the Creator involved considerably more than that. The Lord's intent was that man would *act* like his Maker, and reflect His glory. The likeness would be moral and spiritual, not physical.

Of well-trained animals, such as dogs, horses, and chimpanzees, it is sometimes remarked that they "act almost human." Something is still lacking, however, which eternally distinguishes them from man. It is that difference which gives us a clue to what the image of God means.

Unlike the lower forms of life, man has the power of reason. No one can prove conclusively that animals cannot reason, but it is more likely that they act from instinct or due to external condi-tioning by man. (By instinct we mean a predetermined disposition which motivates action without the use of the will.) Both God and man have a will, the power of reason, the ability to choose. Other forms of life operate by either seasonal control, as in the case of plants, or instinct, as with animals. The fact that man was created free to choose confirms the view that man is superior to the beasts in his ability to reason.

In addition to the powers of thought, man is capable of laughter and tears. While the hyena is said to laugh and the dog to cry, the laughing is not an emotional reaction to a humorous situation nor does the crying actually express itself in visible tears. Again, these are only instinctual reactions. Man, on the other hand, laughs or weeps when he is happy or sad. Both emotional responses are directly related to the human being's powers of thought.

Animals do seem to be capable of making sounds by which they communicate with one another. Only man, however, possesses the keenly developed language which enables him to be understood adequately so as to become a part of a complex society requiring both reason and the expression of it. The many languages and dialects which characterize different cultural groups demonstrate that man is competent to make himself understood in a number of varied and complicated ways.

The inborn ability to transcend oneself is another gift peculiar to mankind. No beast, fish, or fowl ever sets out to better itself. But man is always in the process of self-transcendence. He is continually seeking to improve himself, to achieve some higher plateau of existence. Not satisfied with being just an animal, he engages in the mental, cultural, and spiritual pursuits which will polish and transform him. What a beast becomes, if there is any improvement, is dependent on outside conditioning forces brought to bear on it by man. On the other hand, man can become almost anything he deliberately sets himself to be. The *becoming,* of course, is always controlled by the nature of humanity which does not allow one to become an angel or a god simply because he has a determination to be such.

Certainly, a word should be said about the deathless quality within the human species. Already we have insisted that the Creator is eternal, without beginning or end. Something of this eternal quality has been shared with mankind so that physical death does not terminate our existence, only our fleshly habitation. Once man is created, he never ceases to be. He will continue to exist forever in some form. And this does not imply that he is reincarnated into some future earthly body. On the contrary, it suggests that every man is a unique creature fashioned after God's likeness and that he lives in his own peculiar form of life eternally, an entity not shared with any other creature.

The Trinity

The definitive New Testament doctrine of the Trinity is foreshadowed in the opening chapter of Genesis. A divine dialogue (or trialogue) is described in which the Creator says, "Let *us* make man in *our* image, after *our* likeness" (v. 26). The question is, to whom was God talking? Some have speculated that the angelic hosts were called in on this supreme act of creation. We would have no particular problem here if it were not for the fact that man is not made in the image of the angels (who were also created) but in the image of God, the uncreated Spirit.

The better explanation is that which sees the *Godhead* at work in creation. Father, Son, and Holy Spirit were all included. How could it have been otherwise if there is unity in the being of God? John's prologue reminds us, "In the beginning was the Word, and the Word was with God, and the Word was God" (John 1:1). Christ was there, even as the Spirit which "moved upon the face of the waters." If man is made in the image of God, and Christ is within the original divine pattern, then our Lord Jesus is the perfect manifestation of man; He is the complete human.

Man, the Caretaker

One other thing needs to be said about the creation of man. He was made responsible at once for all of life around him. Furthermore, he was made aware of his responsibility for his own life and conduct. God had commanded the animal kingdom earlier to multiply each after its own kind. But not until man appears does the Lord say anything about sex. The account reads, "Male and female created He them" (v. 27). In the amplified account of man's beginnings recorded in chapter 2, the responsibility of the human pair is made specifically clear, as we shall see shortly.

To man and the beasts of the fields, God gave every plant and tree (save one) for food. Complete physical provision for man had already been made on the third day. The whole earth was a veritable paradise where nothing needed by man was lacking. It is interesting to observe that creation seems to have fallen naturally into a double triad of days, the second completing the first and the first providing for the second. This is quickly seen by comparing the columns below, the first containing days one through three and the second including days four through six.

Triad 1		Triad 2	
Day	Created	Day	Created
1	light	4	sun, moon, stars
2	atmosphere, waters separated	5	fowl, fish
3	dry land, plant life	6	land animals, man

Light, created on the first day, was brought to its specific completion in the heavenly bodies on the fourth. The atmosphere and water, which were separated on the second day, created conditions for the coming of fowl and fish on the fifth day. And the appearance of dry land and growth of plant life on the third day made ready the whole earth for the creation of land animals and man himself on the final day of creation. Indeed, when God surveyed all that He had made . . . "it was very good!" (v. 31)

The seventh day (2:1-3)

With the universe completed according to His original design, the Creator looked over His work and declared everything to be going as planned. Swarms of fish of all sizes filled the vast seas, fowl flew gracefully in mid-heaven, and the land buzzed with the sounds of new life. Sun, moon, stars, and a maze of heavenly bodies—called *host*—whirled and orbited one another in orderly fashion. Plants and trees luxuriantly covered the earth, and man was entering responsibly into his custodial obligations.

With joyous satisfaction in it all, the Creator *rested* on the seventh day. The basic work had been completed and there was opportunity for a divine respite. By this we do not mean to imply that God literally ceased all activity. Nothing could continue for a single moment if God fully ignored it. We only suggest that the initial steps and stages of creation were now finished.

What was good for God would be good for man as well. If man were in the likeness of God, this assumption would be obviously true. For this reason the Lord *hallowed* or sanctified the seventh day as an interval of rest in the midst of the cycle of seven days. The Sabbath was not set apart originally as a time of worship, but as a rest from activity. Naturally, such a day would soon develop into an opportunity for the expression of worship toward the Author of the event.

It is a known fact that many ancient peoples other than the Hebrews observed one day in seven as a hallowed time. Some deduce from this that the Jews borrowed the custom from their pagan neighbors. It is much more probable that all the peoples had inherited their reverence for a day of rest from oral traditions which may have gone all the way back to Adam himself. Each culture would thus have shared in a common acceptance of an original design. One of the bases for the Sabbath law as given to Moses (Ex. 20:11) was the divine rest.

An Amplification of Creation (2:4-25)

The verse divisions in our English Bible are sometimes unfortunate. There were no numerically devised sections known as chapters and verses in the original Hebrew text. In fact, that text did not even have paragraphs, capitalized sentences, or punctuation. Everything literally ran together. Dividing marks, which were later added to make the location of passages easier, were placed carelessly in more than one instance. The first sentence in 2:4, relating to the generations of creation, refers to the seven days previously recorded rather than to that which is about to be related.

Beginning with the second half of verse four, we have what some say is a fully separate story of creation, coming from a document or tradition which is chronologically contradictory to the story in chapter one. Scholars of the JEP school refer to it as J (chapter 1 and the first three-and-a-half verses of chapter 2 being the P tradition). Others are more flexible as to how the fragments were pieced together.

While the chronology of creation is different in chapter two (man's creation is mentioned before either animals or plants in chapter 2), it is quite possible that this is not an important aspect of what the biblical account is trying to do. Chapter one is intent on fixing the creation of everything at a specific point in the seven stages. Chapter two is concerned with something entirely different. It is the purpose of the latter to give an amplification of certain broad statements made in the former. If this view has credence, we do not need to see two distinct traditions at all.

Man's nature (2:4-7)

First, we are given some specifics as to how God created man, since the preceding account made only a general assertion regarding the origin of human life. Here we are told that "God *formed man* of the *dust* of the ground" (v. 7). Earlier information made it clear that the first man was *created* (*bara*) as a distinct act of the Lord which set him off from all other animals. Now the further clarification is given which tells *how* and *of what* material the job was done. We learn that existing earth particles were used to make man and that the Creator shaped or fashioned the ingredients into the physical specimen wanted. This means simply that man was to be an integral part of the world itself, made of native stuff and destined to return to the soil, to give back as much as he had taken out. The forming itself does not suggest manipulative handling but specific and personal care given man by the Creator.

For the first time God is given a personal name, *Jehovah* (Yahweh). Previously only the generic title (God) was used for the Supreme Being. This is the first step in the Creator's progressive revelation of Himself to the world which He had made. Since the personal name characterizes this chapter, some scholars refer to it as the J (for *Jahweh* or the *Judean* prophet responsible) document mentioned in the introduction of this book. Our English Bible translates this personal name as LORD. If the Supreme Being were to take such personal care in creating man as chapter two suggests, we would expect Him to be understood as a personal God. As such, He would certainly possess a name.

Breathing into this earthen vessel the "breath of life" was, according to the Hebrew way of stating it, how the Eternal shared His very life and being with man. The word for *breath* is *ruach,* the same as that for *wind* or *spirit.* Thus we see that the *Spirit* which had earlier moved over the waters now moved over man and took up residence within him. This life-giving Holy Spirit is responsible for the unique nature of man, making him reflect God's nature. This dynamic breath of the Eternal was the same as that which came in another way upon the disciples at Pentecost (Acts 2).

The breath of God should not be confused with man's physically controlled inhaling and exhaling of air. Other animal life does this as well as men. Here it is well to note that the word translated "a living soul" (v. 7), is *nephesh* and means "a complete person." The same word is used to describe the animals as "living creatures" and indicates that man and animal alike share what the Hebrews called "soul" (*nephesh*). It is not man's soul which makes him different from the animal world around him but his spirit (*ruach*).* While some scholars insist that this is no implication of a distinct difference in man over other animal life, to be *breathed into* by God carries with it the idea of being especially endued with a quality of being which is beyond physical existence. This was the place, time, and manner of man's reception of the *image* or *likeness* of God.

The Garden of Eden (2:8-17)

Second, the amplification of the creation story gives further details

---

* An excellent treatment of this distinctiveness in the human is found in J. Stafford Wright's *Mind, Man and the Spirits* (Grand Rapids: Zondervan, 1971), pp. 146-156.

about the kind of place prepared in the midst of the whole world for man to live. Iife began for mankind in a *garden,* and it will find its culmination in a similar place (Rev. 21—22). Both the first and the last garden are described in paradisal terms as being fully adequate for man's need and abundant in their luscious provisions. The garden was *planted* by God with every good and pleasant tree and plant to bear fruit for use of the man whom He had created and placed there. Whatever the original garden of Eden may have been before sin entered to defile it, the cleansed earth will be similar after the return of Christ and the coming of the new age.

Scripture describes the area where man began his garden adventure. The names of the Tigris and Euphrates Rivers are familiar to everyone and give the first important clue. The Pison and Gihon Rivers were probably ancient canals which formed connections between the two major rivers. This would have created a river valley conducive to the existence of such a primitive settlement. The biblical description coincides with the opinions of modern science as to the place where civilization began. Man's original earthly home was somewhere in the basin of the eastern Mediterranean and the land lying to the east in proximity to it. Apparently the garden was rich in mineral resources and provided an ideal climate for the growth of vegetation.

In the midst of the many trees which grew in the garden were two special ones called "the tree of life" and "the tree of the knowledge of good and evil." From the beginning of time, life has been in a state of tension. If man were to share the Creator's likeness, he must be allowed the use of his will. Where there is no choice, will is not only superfluous but nonexistent. Only in the midst of creative tension which provides at least one option can man be other than a non-choosing beast. The continual conflict made possible by the presence of a choice between two alternatives is an essential ingredient in responsible living.

Explicit instructions were given by God to man as to where his human rights ended. He was clearly warned against partaking of the "tree of the knowledge of good and evil." Everything else was his, including the "tree of life." This is not to say that man *could* not eat of the forbidden fruit, but that he *should* not do so in view of the consequences which would follow. To do so was to disobey the Creator and to take matters completely into man's hands without regard to either God's love or His wrath. In effect, it was to declare oneself independent of divine supervision and capable of self-sufficiency. More will be said about this matter in the section dealing with the fall of man into sin. Suffice it to say at this point that the Lord did not leave man in the dark regarding the ultimate tragedy of disobedience. Disregard of divine guidance could result in nothing less than death.

Man's other self (2:18-25)

Third, the creation of man, who is described in chapter one simply as "male and female," is now explained. We learn the reason for and method of creation of the female complement. The stated reason relates to the undesirable state of aloneness. Everything which had been made, the Creator had pronounced *good*. For the first time we now hear Him declaring something otherwise. "It is not good," He said, "for the man to be alone" (see 2:18). Man needed companionship and communication with other creatures similar to himself. Therefore, the Lord formed the creatures of the earth and the air out of the same basic ingredients which had been used for the creation of man. At this point it sounds as though the animals were not created until after man, but the chronological sequence is of little consequence since that is not the point. The animals could have been made before man (as in chapter one) and later brought into his presence to be classified.

The significant thing is that man was given the task of fitting proper names to each species of the animal kingdom, a further indication of his superiority and dominance over them. Since it was man who had to live with his fellow creatures on the earth, God offered no objection to his decisions but permitted his choice of names to stand. While the naming process was a sizeable chore for such a new master-creature, apparently the Creator's purpose was to acquaint man with the living things around him sufficiently to choose one of them as his special companion. In view of the fact that God cannot be surprised, the failure to find a suitable companion may have disappointed man but it did not catch God unprepared.

Under a divinely induced anesthetic which put man to sleep, the Lord continued His creative activity by performing the first surgical operation. Since nothing which had been made was *fit* for man, the only reasonable thing to do was to create his *helper* from his own body. In this way the female would be a part of the male and would share his likeness to the Eternal Spirit, who had breathed into him His own life. From the rib of the man, a helper was fashioned which could well be called man's *alter ego* (other self). When the surgery was completed, God brought the female to man as the animals had been before her, and asked that a name be provided for the new creature.

Immediately, the man recognized her as being more like himself than any beast or fowl which he had named. Unquestionably, something about her spirit must have implied that she also shared in a relationship with the Creator which had thus far been unique to the man alone. At last he had looked upon his own flesh and bones, a likeness of himself which pleased him and was fully acceptable. Without hesitation he gave her a name which not only would identify her in the midst of lesser creatures, but which put her into the human arena as an integral part of the Lord God's masterpiece. She would be called *woman* (*ishshah*) because she was taken out of *man* (*ish*).

No relationship in the world is so cohesive as that which exists between a man and a woman. So binding is it that, at the outset of creation, God emphasized the responsibility involved in the co-habitation of the two parts of the generic species called *man*. At no place are we told that the Creator made a like demand upon any other creature. The beasts, fowl, and fish were commanded to *reproduce* but without restrictions except that each should breed with its own kind. Man, however, was restricted to his *alter ego,* his sole female counterpart, with whom he was *one flesh.* Man and woman belong together, but not man and women or woman and men. The biological and spiritual tie is so strong and permanently designed that the relationship becomes even stronger than that between a child and his parents. Even at this early stage of human history, the institution of marriage was divinely sanctioned.

An almost parenthetical word is added regarding the nakedness of the new couple and their unashamedness. Of all God's creatures, only man wears clothing. Undoubtedly our wearing apparel may be made decorative and colorful, but it is due to man's sin. Any contemporary emphasis on the sanctity of the body and a return to nudity is a counterfeit effort on the part of sinful man to act like primordial innocents. Nudity is not in the divine plan for the present age, as is evidenced by God's provision of skin tunics (3:21). Man exists in a state of sinfulness. Only where there is sinlessness or innocence, as in the lower animal kingdom, does nudity become a wholesome way of life.

Prior to the fall of the Edenic couple, they were unashamed of their nakedness. Living in a fresh world of untainted perfection, the man and woman shared in the holiness of creation. The innocence of the new world lent itself to unimpaired communication between man and other creatures, between man and his alter ego, and between man and his Creator.

2
THE FALL
OF MAN

Genesis 3:1—4:26

So far in the creation story we have seen only three featured actors: God the Creator, man the created, and woman. And she has thus far remained silent! Actually only God and man have played roles requiring more than bare appearances. Neither the animals nor woman speak or perform in any definite manner until the opening of chapter three. Then the woman gets into the act, and a fourth personage, the serpent, assumes a prominent place.

Interpretations of the serpent run the full gamut of possibilities from that of an actual, slithering snake to an imaginary and fictitous character in an old folktale. There is little question that symbolism is used in Genesis, even as it is in The Revelation. Certainly, regardless of what symbolism if any is used here, Satan could become incarnate in a serpent or take the appearance of a snake. The spirit world is continually impinging on the physical. Indeed, the physical and spirit worlds may not be nearly so far apart or exclusive of one another as we sometimes think. Jesus emphatically states that Satan entered into Judas Iscariot (see John 13:27). If the devil could inhabit the body of a disciple of Jesus, what would keep him from taking up temporary residence in the skin of a snake?

Nothing is said in the creation story about Satan, but the serpent is identified in Revelation 12:9. Even Jesus spoke of Satan's existence "from the beginning" (John 8:44). The Revelation portrays him as a *dragon* (serpent) who will spectacularly appear again at

31

the end of the present age to deceive as he did earlier in the garden. He who appears as "an angel of light" (2 Cor. 11:14) in the New Testament also appeared in the form of a serpent in the Old Testament. He always assumes whatever likeness is necessary to accomplish his purposes.

The woman was familiar with every kind of creature and friendly with all creation before sin disrupted the paradise of God. There was no reason not to trust the serpent whose suggestion seemed as reasonable to the woman as Satan's temptations seem logical to us.

The Seduction (3:1-6)

The modern mind is immediately suspicious of fantasy when a serpent speaks. A lot of jokes are based on this scene in Genesis, let alone sincere theological discussions. We are just not accustomed to communicating with serpents in intelligent conversation. The voice which came from the body of the serpent, however, was not its own.

During the ministry of Jesus, demons which were in possession of men's bodies spoke quite distinctly. One who lived among the tombs was possessed by so many of Satan's demonic forces that the spokesman named himself *Legion* (Mark 5:9; Luke 8:30). Another instance of talking demons is found in Mark 1:24, where the devilish tenant in a man cried out to Jesus, "I know who You are—the Holy One!" (Luke 4:34, NASB). The serpent could be an instrument of Satan as easily as a man.

It's always risky business to enter into dialogue with Satan. He is "more subtle than any other." It was because of his subtle, yet brazen, attempt to overthrow the Lord God and take His throne that he was cast out of heaven long before the creation of man (Isaiah 14:12-14; see also Luke 10:18). This acounts for his presence in the garden, in possession of a newly-made serpent's body, when man appeared. The fact that he existed at all is to be understood only if it is remembered that God had created him as an angel among the celestial servants of the Eternal. Because of his former state, he found it easy to appear as an angel of light or an unsuspected creature of subtlety—much better to deceive us that way!

The conversation was opened by the servant. That's typical, since the devil takes the initiative whenever possible. It is also in keeping with his subtle nature to put his temptations in the form of suggestion (here a suggestive question) rather than an abrupt, obvious affront. His strategy makes much of deceptive tactics which catch the seduced person off guard.

Satan's approach to the subject was done in such a way as to create a "positive" rather than a negative atmosphere. The first question was to make it clear that the Creator had given the couple much more permissiveness than they might have thought! Satan was suggesting that it was perfectly obvious that God had not withheld *any* tree except one and, since there was no visible difference, it was probably a joke being played on some very naïve people!

By this time Satan was in a position to help the woman rationalize the whole thing in such a manner as to make God's rule seem a bit ridiculous. Certainly, Satan wanted her to think that just eating of the "tree of the knowledge of good and evil" would not bring so severe a penalty as death. The Creator would not be so rash as to destroy what He had made for so little a thing as "forbidden fruit."

With such beautiful satanic logic making its point in her subconscious, the woman was prepared for the next devilish suggestion. "It should be perfectly clear to you," insisted the serpent, "that the Creator is only protecting Himself against your sharing in His wisdom. He knows full well that the fruit from the tree will enlighten you. You will know good and evil. You will be like God Himself!"

Satan was correct in his assurance that man, by disobedience, would know *both* good and evil. The distortion lay in the fact that such a result was made to look like a blessing when it was actually a curse. Until the woman partook of the forbidden tree, neither she nor Adam knew sin. They experienced only good. Becoming acquainted with evil would not enhance their situation one bit. It would only complicate and frustrate their existence. For while it would make them wise, a "man and woman of the world," it would destroy their innocence and ruin their rapport with the One who had made them.

The "benefit" of disobedience was far too costly ever to be considered a bargain, the serpent's logic notwithstanding.

Nothing could be more in keeping with the nature of the Evil One than the obsession to be *like God*. This desire and the action to fulfil it, was what cost Satan his place among the angels. Having watched his plan abort, he had only one thing left. If the serpent could get God's most valued creature to carry out the personal ambition of Satan, the archenemy of the Lord would save face and achieve success. Therefore, the voice from the snake promised the woman that rebellion would make her *like God*.

What the voice did not make clear was that such rebel action had resulted in Satan's expulsion from the celestial world and would likewise force Adam and Eve out of their garden paradise. In addition, it would estrange the creature from the Creator just as it had brought about enmity between Satan and the Lord God.

In reality, if man were to be like God at all, it would come about by eating of the other tree—"the tree of life"—which was synonymous with obedience. Man grows more like God by obeying Him and less like Him when disobedient.

Seeing how beautiful the forbidden tree looked, how satisfying its fruit appeared, and how much it pleased the aspiring ego, the woman chose to experiment with the only thing that she had been flatly denied. Desirous of being a good *helpmeet* (one fit to be the man's wife), she withheld nothing of her discovery from her companion. Perhaps there may have been also an unconscious fear of the consequences and an effort to involve another in her deed. In this way, she would not have to face the Creator's anger alone—if He would indeed react that way!

So the two of them together smugly shared the forbidden fruit. Then they waited for the promised metamorphosis which would make them *like God!*

Hardly.

The Tragic Consequences of Disobedience (3:7-24)

What a surprise awaited the erring pair. The shock was almost too much for their untempered beings. Indeed, their eyes were opened and they "wisely" observed their own nakedness. This is probably a picturesque way of saying that the divine effulgence which had surrounded them was suddenly lost. The nature clothing which belonged to their human innocence and perfection was taken away. They were left staring at each other's bodies, which were shorn of purity.

At once the couple began to realize that there are possibilities of evil in everything, and that precautions must be taken lest their new "enlightenment" become their total ruin.

This is not to say that there was anything wrong with sex as God had created it. From the beginning man was "male and female" and told to "multiply" his seed. But with the original disobedience came the power to misuse everything which had been created. In recognition of this possibility, the man and woman made fig-leaf coverings for their stark nakedness.

Conscious that there would be a confrontation with their Maker, the man and his mate hid in the undergrowth of the garden. When God appeared to them, the man admitted that he was afraid to come into the open. His fear was related to his nakedness. Whatever had happened, he knew that both he and his companion were different than when they last had communicated with the Lord.

The divine question, "Who told you that you were naked?" reveals the awesome truth that sin brings its own consciousness. No one needs be told he is guilty. Within every man there exists that haunting awareness. And though we may not admit our own sinfulness, God knows of it and is fully aware of what has brought about our fearful shame. That which had happened to the human pair was precisely what God knew would happen if they disobeyed. He knew that the foolish pair had tampered with the one thing He had denied them.

Human nature has changed very little. We still have a spontaneous reaction to our guilt. We still look for ways of escaping our responsibility by shifting the blame from ourselves. Sometimes we make heredity the scapegoat, but more often it is environment. Man argues that he cannot help himself. Either his parents are to blame or his world has let him down. Whichever it is that has done him in, he insists that he is not accountable.

Both the man and the woman laid the blame on their environment. The man accused the woman of leading him astray, and the woman accused the serpent. Since blaming the woman was like accusing his *alter ego,* man was really admitting unknowingly his own composite guilt.

Since the serpent had initiated the fall of man, he was first to be reprimanded and punished. A divine curse was placed upon him, reducing him to a thing of horrendous appearance. The snake was to be cursed "above all the cattle, and above all wild animals." Clearly the implied suggestion is that the serpent was originally a part of the *walking* animal kingdom, for now he was cursed to crawl upon his *belly.*

There was a further punishment, however, promised not so much to the serpent as to the devil who had used the snake as an instrument of evil. Henceforth, the offspring of the woman and that of the serpent would be mortal enemies. A visible reminder of this prediction is to be seen in the usual revulsion felt toward any serpent, especially by women. But the more penetrating prophecy has to do with the continuous conflict between Satan and Christ, referred to here as "her seed." This early promise of God assures us of both a lifelong battle with the devil and of his final undoing in the age to come.

While the bruising of Christ was witnessed in His death on the cross, it was not fatal—as the expression "bruise his heel" would imply. Christ was to live again. But the bruising of the serpent (Satan) is to be a mortal wound, suggested by the expression "bruise thy head." This is more fully described in Revelation 20:10.

Glad to see the serpent get what he deserved, the human couple probably felt relieved. But only for a moment. To the woman, God promised two consequences of this fall: total subjection to her husband, and pain in bearing children. Apparently, the reproduction of the human race would have had no relationship to discomfort of any kind if the woman had not sinned. But now it was to involve travail.

To the man, God promised a life of hard labor. Work itself is not part of the curse since the Creator labored for six days and placed man in the garden to "till and keep it." The punishment lay rather in the discomfort which would accompany man's labor in the future. The ground itself would be cursed so that its production would be determined by man's work in the "sweat of his brow."

Obvious effects of the divine punishment are to be seen in the pains of childbirth and the ease with which the ground produces weeds.

Adam, which is not used in the English transliteration until Genesis 2:19, was not originally a proper name. It was an equivalent English spelling of a Hebrew sound. The word means *man* and is not altered at Genesis 2:19 in the Hebrew from the word previously employed. *Adam* is a shortened form of *adamah* (ground) and seems to suggest that man is an *earthling,* made of the dust and destined to return to it (3:19).

A Forecast of Salvation

The Hebrew word which Adam gave to his wife at this point was *Eve (hawwah)* meaning *life-giver*. Perhaps this is the place to note that the earlier reference to the Christ (her seed) is in complete agreement with the biblical account of the birth of Christ by a virgin. The woman is the mother of all life and, in this specific instance, the offspring was described as *her* seed and not that of a man also.

There is a beautiful picture of God's salvation from our sins here. God's making "garments of skin" to clothe Adam and Eve must be understood in the light of their having earlier clothed themselves with fig-leaf aprons. Fig-leaf material was fragile and subject to deterioration, so something more substantial was needed. The picture is that man's attempt at covering up the reality of his sin is always inadequate. We cannot redeem the situation by anything that we may do. Only God, who made man, can provide the proper "covering" for his sin and shame.

Skins show the necessity of the slaying of animals since such covering could be derived in no other way. And this makes clear the use of sacrificial blood in covering man's sin. It may be that this was the time when God instituted the sacrificial system of atonement elaborately developed in a later period. Certainly the use of skins pointed to the hour when man's sin problem would be handled once-and-for-all in the death of Christ, the Lamb of God.

A "conference" held among the Trinity sought to deal with the matter of man's having "become like one of us." The next words forbid our thinking of man as becoming *like God* in any other way except in his discernment of good and evil. Like God, they knew good and evil, but unlike God, they were disposed *toward the evil*. Lest Adam should eat of the "tree of life," which had earlier been accessible to him, and live forever in his state of self-perpetuating evil, the decision was reached to expel the couple from the garden. Adam and Eve were destined to live totally removed from the given source of their divine life.

Angels guarded the entrance to the garden and its life-giving tree. If man were to find a path of return to God, the Lord Himself would have to provide that way. From this point in the story of the beginnings of human life there unfolds before us God's dramatic plan of redemption for the man whose divine image had been distorted by sin.

Original Sin Bears Bitter Fruit (4:1-24)

Outside the garden of Eden, Eve gave birth to a son whom Adam named Cain. The name may mean no more than one *gotten* from the Creator or it may mean *smith,* which some say is an insight into the work with iron which later proved to be his descendants' contribution to the society.

No question existed in Eve's mind about where the child had come from; she had gotten him "with the help of the Lord." God had not abandoned them even though the pair had sinned. His proceeding with the creation of additional human life meant that He would eventually work out His plan.

The Hebrew states that Adam *knew* Eve and she conceived. The word *know* is still used today to describe sexual experience. The one who is accused of having been intimate with a minor is said to have "carnal knowledge." To *know* Eve meant that Adam experienced the very essence of her being and shared completely in her life.

Abel, who may have been Cain's twin, means *breath,* which may have something to do with the shortness of his existence.

Cain was a farmer and Abel a shepherd. One task was not more sacred to God than the other. God had explicitly stated that man was to both "have dominion" over all animal life and "till and keep" the ground. That is, man was responsible for both the animal and the plant kingdom. Cain assumed one role and Abel the other.

Where Cain made his mistake was not in being a farmer but in offering a sacrifice of herbs and plants rather than a sacrifice of blood. Though we are not specifically told, it is rather obvious that Cain knew of God's preference for animal sacrifice. The Creator may have explained the sacrificial system to Adam when He made the skins to cover his nakedness. "In process of time" (v. 3), it appears that the two sons would have understood what God demanded. Cain could have easily traded his fruits to Abel for a lamb or some other suitable animal. For Cain to come to the place of sacrifice with the wrong kind of offering strongly implied that there was something defiant in his attitude. This may be accounted for by the proneness to sin engendered in him by his parents. We call this man's "Adamic nature"—he is spiritually bent out of shape! Paul dwells on it at length in his letter to the Romans (5:12-21).

The Lord's warning to Cain that sin was "couching at the door" and that he "must master it" rather than succumb to it seemed to do little good. The voice of God was heeded no more than it had been by his father before him. In cold premeditation, he lured his brother away from the family and the place of sacrifice and killed him.

Thus, right from the beginning, man despised the two basic principles upon which all life must exist: he refused to love God above all else (Adam's fall) and he refused to love his brother as himself (Cain's sin). The Law and Jesus' later summarization of it (Mark 12:29-31) had not yet been given, but the fabric of creation itself is woven upon these two fundamentals.

As Adam's sin against his Maker separated him from God, so Cain's sin against his brother resulted in the same spiritual death. In the first instance, the Lord asked Adam, "Where are you?" And in the second He said to Cain, "Where is your brother?" In both cases man had been responsible for moving away from the Creator. In the dawn of human life, man defied first his God and then his brother, all in the effort to become his own master and pursue life his own way.

Now Cain receives the inevitable—punishment for sin. No longer would he be a farmer. The blood of his brother had soaked into the ground, which would react by not producing for the murderer. The future days of Cain would be spent in wandering across the earth as a fugitive. This curse was not to a nomadic life but to one of constant running without the benefit of a stabilizing culture.

Looking at the lonely future, Cain cried because of the severity of the punishment. How much better it would have been to weep over his monstrous guilt!

God always tempers His judgment in mercy. Lest men be too anxious to kill Cain, a divine mark (we know not what it was) was placed on him to identify and protect him. "The land of Nod" (exile) was most likely an outlying and somewhat desolate area.

Mention of Cain's wife (4:17) is an abrupt intrusion into the story. Perhaps he took a wife immediately after receiving his sentence due to his fear of being alone in a hostile world. Since olden times the question of where he found a wife has been debated. Some insist that Adam was a race of people rather than one man. However, the most likely solution is that Cain married his sister. Already he has admitted his fear that men would kill him, so obviously there were other people on the earth. They were probably other sons and daughters, maybe grandchildren, of Adam and Eve. Tradition has come down to us that God's first man had 33 sons and 27 daughters. Genesis does state that he had "other sons and daughters" (5:4).

Cain's son was named *Enoch*—"dedicated." A city named for him was begun in the land of Nod. This could well have been Cain's way of trying to compensate for his sin by dedicating his firstborn to the Lord. Tradition again hints at the vague possibility that the city which Cain built was never completed, which if true would confirm God's sentence—he would be a wandering fugitive. Of Cain's desperate plight which led him to originate the city, Jacques Ellul prophetically states, "He no longer believes in this God who seems to have condemned him because he had supremely insulted Him. So Cain has no way of knowing that this mark (which he cannot see) will suffice to protect him, even in the depth of his sin, from his disobedience, from his separation from God. And now Cain will spend his life trying to find security, struggling against hostile forces, dominating men and nature, taking guarantees that are within his reach, guarantees that *appear* to him to be genuine, but which in fact protect him from nothing." *

Nine descendants of Cain are mentioned before we lose track of his family. Of those nine we know nothing except what little is sandwiched into the brief statement about Lamech and his offspring. What an example of how sin can go from bad to worse in a family like Cain's. Lamech appears, in the poetic song he composed, to have outdone his murderous ancestor by killing young and old at the least provocation. "For any who wounded me, him have I slain, also the young man, who gave me a scratch" (4:23, BERK). Furthermore, Lamech is the first polygamist, having married two wives in spite of the Creator's emphatic statement that *one* man and *one* woman form one flesh.

We learn that the children born to these unions were musicians, in the case of Jubal, and workers of iron, in the case of Tubalcain. This information reveals that men began to use metals while Adam was yet alive. Some scholars still insist that metals could not have been used in the ancient beginning of human life, but

---

* Jacques Ellul, *The Meaning of the City* (Grand Rapids, Eerdmans, 1970), pp. 2-3. Ellul's book is a superb interpretation of the origin, existence, and destiny of the city as man's act of self-sufficiency and God-displacement. Although one may not be able to accept the author's tendency to "over-spiritualize" at points, his contribution to an understanding of the God-denying city is most illuminating.

archaeologists are continually discovering fragments of iron, copper, and bronze which predate the latest established chronology.

A Ray of Hope (4:25-26)

At that exact moment when things appear to be at their worst, God intervenes with a renewal of hope. Abel was dead and the descendants of Cain grew increasingly degenerate. The author of the creation story terminates the genealogy of Cain with Lamech's immediate family. There was no point in looking further for a God-fearing line—it just was not going to develop among the Cainites. Therefore, the creation account turns its focus in another direction, to the birth of a new son to Adam and Eve. His name was *Seth,* meaning *appointed.* Eve was sure that this son had been appointed to fill the vacancy of Abel and offset the terrible blight which Cain had added to the family.

To Seth was born a son who was given the name *Enos.* With him, at last, things began to change. Men began to call on the name of the Lord, to invoke His name in prayer. Cain's descendants were to become renowned for ironwork, poetry, and music. Seth's children were known for their practice of worship, their deepening piety, and their communication with the Creator. Since spirit is more enduring than flesh, the household of Seth continues in favor with God and man to this day, long after that of Cain has passed into oblivion.

3
THE PATRIARCH PROCESSION

Genesis 5:1-32

The genealogical account in this chapter is partly repetitious since it goes back over the generations of Adam as well as introducing some new personalities who figured in the story of the beginnings. Undoubtedly, only the most important men were listed. The others were of so little consequence in the divine program that even their names are lost. Not that there were no good men among them, but such an account could only mention the most spectacular out of the multitude to march across the stage of primitive history.

These people lived to be extremely old! How? It may be that these ancients did not calculate time in the same manner we do today. Some think that the lengthy life-span was not that of a single person but the accumulated years of the members of his family. But there is little reason, on the other hand, to doubt the actual and literal durability of human life. In the infancy of creation before sin had complicated life by the many diseases and scourges which afflict us today, man may have lived several times as long as we do.

Only 10 fathers of the race are listed in this one chapter, though there may have been many names which could have been included. What we have before us, however, is the genealogy of the family of Adam as that line of descent bears upon the future.

An Explanation of Confusion (4:17-18; 5:13-25)

Some scholars say that the genealogy of Cain in chapter four is so similar to that of Seth in chapter five that we probably have two separate traditions which became confused in the process of being handed down through the generations. This is not necessarily so. Several alternatives are possible. The names in question are *Enoch, Irad, Mehujael, Methuselah,* and *Lamech* in chapter four—the descendants of Cain, and *Mahalalel, Jared, Enoch, Methuselah,* and *Lamech*—offspring from the line of Seth listed in chapter five.

First, we should note that the order in each line of descent is not the same. *Enoch* is first among the five in Cain's line and third in Seth's. This makes the former Enoch a great-grandfather of one named Methuselah and the other Enoch a father. The spelling of *Jared* and *Irad* may indicate two different persons rather than word corruption. The same thing is true of *Mehujael* and *Mahalalel.* It may also be observed that the direct descent of these two pairs of names is in reverse order. All this would suggest that we may have a perfectly correct rendering of the names of distinct descendants in two separate family lines.

Second, even if it could be shown that the two lists of names and the order of descent were identical, we have still not proved the two lines were confused. Even today brothers are known to have children with the same names. More distantly removed descendants such as grandchildren and great grandchildren are even more likely to have identical names.

And could it not be that Seth, the one appointed to continue the creation begun in Adam by God, was naming his offspring with the names which had been disgraced by Cain's line? May he not have been saying that Enoch could be a godly man, Methuselah could count for something in God's plan, and Lamech could produce life rather than death? In fact, the grandson of Seth was *Kenan* (an Anglicized form of Cainan), possibly an attempt to prove that even the name *Cain* could be redeemed. God was "start-over again" in Seth's line, as He was later to do with Noah's family following the flood.

A Man Who Walked With God (5:18-24)

Though only a few lines are devoted to him, Enoch is one of the most famous men in the Old Testament. We remember and respect him because he proved to his contemporaries, in a time when the Adamic curse was still fresh in the mind of everyone, that one could "walk with God" as Adam did before his sin. The life of

Enoch was evidence that the Creator was concerned about man and that He had not forsaken His world. God was continually near enough for communication and companionship with man.

When Enos lived (4:26) the world *began* to call upon the name of the Lord, but not until many generations later did God find one who would actually *walk* with Him. For 300 years, Enoch had fellowship with God similar to that which Adam knew prior to the fall.

Enoch had a privilege only one other person has had. He and Elijah were both permitted entrance into the world to come without passing through the usual experience of death. Concisely and with great emphasis it is recorded, "Enoch walked with God; and he was not, for God took him" (v. 24). Elijah's *translation* is recorded in 2 Kings 2:11-12.

The word which is used to describe Enoch's going away (translation) has two meanings: to be exalted into a state of rapture, and to bypass death. Both these definitions throw light on what happened. Enoch lived in such constant communion with God that he finally reached a state of spiritual ecstasy and, in the midst of it, was caught up to be with the angelic hosts. His fellowship with the Lord was such that his translation from one world to another was probably not that big a switch spiritually. But it was quite a reward physically! The writer of Hebrews lists a host of men who lived and conquered by faith—Enoch is among them (11:5).

When Christ returns, the Church will be translated like this man of faith in the Old Testament. He was raptured from this world to the next without death (1 Thes. 4:13-18). The rapture of the Church, when Christ comes for His saints, will become a reality for those who are *in the faith*. Man walks with God by faith alone, not by sight, and our entrance into the world to come will be determined by the presence or absence of saving faith in Jesus Christ. We enter the true Church here by faith, not by works, and we will someday enter the new heaven an dearth on the basis of that same faith.

As the translation of Enoch reminded his contemporaries of the blessed life after death, so it must have had within it some hint of the coming flood of judgment upon wickedness. Likewise, the Rapture of the Church will remind the world that there is another life beyond this parenthesis in time and that judgment will soon fall upon an unbelieving world.

An Incarnate Prophecy (5:25-27)

Hardly anyone sees anything worth discussing about Methuselah. People know his name because he lived longer than anyone else. Because of this he has become the butt of numerous jokes—the man who lived almost 1,000 years and did absolutely nothing! And supposedly this is a correct appraisal of his life so far as his recorded works are concerned.

But there is more here than meets the eye. Ancient men were given names descriptive of what they were hoped to become or names suggesting some characteristic of their lives. "Methuselah" is one of the most intriguing names in the Old Testament. It would appear that God may have led Enoch in naming his son. At any rate, He must have explained to him what the prophetic sign connected with his son was all about.

"Methuselah" probably means *when gone, so be it*. God was informing Enoch and the world of his time that something was going to happen of worldwide significance at the time of Methuselah's death. What was it? The following chapter recounts the story of the Flood. Noah was the grandson of Methuselah, who was 187 years old when Lamech, Noah's father, was born. Lamech was 182 years old at the birth of Noah. This means that Methuselah was 369 years of age when his grandson was born. Now Noah is said to have been 600 years old when the Flood came. If the age of Methuselah at the birth of Noah (369) is added to Noah's age at the beginning of the flood (600, according to Gen. 7:6), the accumulated years are 969. The flood came when Methuselah was 969, which is just how old he was when he died! Hence, God must have been saying to Enoch that Methuselah would be an incarnate prophecy of the great deluge, a sign to the antediluvian (before the Flood) world of the approach of judgment.

Some, who reject the note of prophecy in Scripture, insist that these figures are not important except to indicate that Methuselah was drowned in the Flood itself. This explanation sounds good at first. It would seem after more careful study, however, that having been given a name which meant *when gone, so be it,* he probably died the year of the Flood but sometime before it as a last-minute warning to the men and women of his day to prepare for the deluge.

This would account for his exceedingly long life as well. While nothing he did was recorded, he nevertheless lived nearly a millennium, due to the mercy and longsuffering of God, who was giving the people every opportunity for repentance.

This may also account for the statement, "Enoch walked with God *after* the birth of Methuselah 300 years" (see 5:22). It was perhaps not until his son was born and the significance of his name was made plain that Enoch began to live in constant fellowship with the Lord.

4
GOD
BEGINS AGAIN

Genesis 6:1—9:29

The Creator had instructed Adam and Eve to multiply, to reproduce until the new world was filled with people like themselves. By the time of Noah the command had been carried out to such a degree that the earth was beginning to be filled with thousands of human beings—men and women, boys and girls.

Cohabitation was taking place, sometimes with the controls of legal marriage, but too often purely on the basis of physical attraction. Wives were taken because they "were fair" to look upon. Neither ancient nor modern marriage can be expected to be permanent or meaningful when entered into on the basis of bodily desire alone.

Unequal Yokes (6:1-4)

Genesis 6 mentions two groups of people who "married" one another—the "sons of God" and the "daughters of men." A theory widely held is that the former were angels who cohabited with the female offspring of fallen people. Such passages as 2 Peter 2:4 and Jude 6-7 are usually cited for support of this idea. But these references more likely speak of the fall of the angels who rebelled with Lucifer (Satan) long before the appearance of man on earth. Jesus clearly stated that angels do not marry (the word in the Genesis passage connotes a married state), which would imply that they are sexless and that sexual intercourse would be impossible for them (Mark 12:25).

47

A better explanation is that the "sons of God" were descendants of Seth and the "daughters of men" were the offspring of Cain. Earlier mention was made relating to Seth's having been *appointed* by God to take the place of Abel. We have already seen how wicked the generations of Cain became and how those of Seth began to call on the name of the Lord (Gen. 4:26).

If the "sons of God" were Sethites, then this passage describes a normal marriage agreed upon by a male and female, both of the human species. The tragedy of it was that the line of Seth, on whom the Creator was depending to help create a God-honoring world, was becoming enamored with the obviously Satan-controlled line of Cain. Such a union could produce nothing but more wickedness and disaster. And that is exactly what happened.

The offspring of the union of God's people with Satan's were called *Nephilim* (v. 4). These creatures are often supposed to be giants of some kind who ruled with a big hand. But this need not be the case. To be called "mighty men" (rendered *giants* in the King James Version) does not imply physical size anymore than it suggests mental and worldly prowess. In fact, they were also plainly called "men of renown."

The alternative possibility is to translate the word itself as *assaulters*. That would be in keeping with the nature of the Cainite line, which was known for its murder and vicious hostility. Whatever the Nephilim may have been, they were so ruthlessly wicked and corrupt that the Creator allowed only 120 years before they were totally and irrevocably destroyed. The 120 years does not refer to a maximum age span for man (some post-Flood patriarchs lived longer) but to an allotted "time of grace" before judgment in the Flood.

One in a Thousand (6:5—8:19)
Having become so depraved that his thoughts and imaginations were "evil continually," man was finally destined to be destroyed. Animals and fowl would also perish. Man's excessive wickedness had obviously contaminated everything he touched.

It is unimportant but interesting to note that the fish, which could swim in the Flood, are not mentioned as suffering from man's sinfulness. Possibly this is because man was a creature of the land and had not extended his godless influence beyond that point.

In the big mess of human wickedness which covered the whole ancient world, God found one man who would *walk* with Him—Noah. It was reminiscent of Enoch, Noah's great-grandfather.

Large numbers of scholars continue to reject the biblical story of the Flood. The whole thing is said to be an old myth which cannot be supported with sound evidence. Naturally it is difficult to prove anything which happened so far in the distant past, long before recorded history.

Jesus, however, spoke of the Flood as an historical fact (Matt. 24:37-39). And of course He was around when it happened!

An interesting support, a flood story is to be found in the traditions of all peoples: Babylonians, Assyrians, Egyptians, Greeks, Chinese, Aryans, Persians, Polynesians, Celts, Incas, ad infinitum. In every case only one family is said to have escaped in some kind of floating device. The universality of the story simply supports the fact that, at some ancient date, the Flood of Genesis did take place. Additional evidence has been discovered in actual layers of mud excavated at such interesting places as Ur (only a few miles from the site of Eden), Fara (where the Babylonian Noah is said to have lived), and Kish (a number of miles to the north).

In light of the stratified condition of the earth, flood geologists argue a universal deluge which submerged the world and transformed it into an entierly different thing than what it was before the Flood. Fossil bones of animals, birds, and sea creatures are found stratified in rock far away from their native habitats. If there were no other reasons for believing that Noah's flood covered the whole world, this one fact should give us a pause in our reflections!

Due to the corruption of all flesh, God warned Noah that the Flood was coming and gave him 120 years to prepare a great ship (ark) for the saving of his family and every species of created animal life. During this time Noah was also to preach (prophesy) to the pagan culture, that they might have adequate warning.

Specific instructions were given as to the size and method of constructing the ark. When the cubits are converted into feet, the ark comes out approximately 500 feet long, 75 feet wide, and 50 feet high. This would mean that there were several floor levels (three according to v. 16), which greatly expanded the space needed for so large a number of animals. The ship was to be constructed of gopher wood (an unknown type) and covered on the inside and outside with pitch to seal it. The interior was to be well furnished with food and stocked with all necessities needed for such a voyage.

A pair of all unclean animals was taken into the ark to prevent their extinction. Seven pairs of all clean animals and fowl were taken aboard because of the need for animal sacrifice and for animal food for man, which would be allowed following the Flood. In addition to the menagerie of animals, Noah was instructed to take seven passengers besides himself—his wife, his three sons, and their wives.

"The fountains of the great deep burst forth" (7:11, NASB), meaning the rivers and oceans overflowed their basins to which they had long been restricted by the Creator. The windows of the heavens were opened. The water above the firmament (atmospheric, cloudy moisture) came down in great force to help overflow the pools of earthbound water. For 40 days and nights the rains fell. The rivers soon swelled far beyond their banks as the ark tossed violently with its godly family and odorous zoo.

The area where human life was concentrated—the Near East—was inundated from all sides, being surrounded by the Indian Ocean, the Mediterranean, and the Caspian, Black, and Arabian Seas. The whole race was destroyed. Whether humans yet lived outside the general area of earliest man is unknown. If they did, then the whole earth had to be covered with water to accomplish man's total destruction.

According to the scriptural account, the floods rose about 20 feet above the highest mountains. Mount Ararat,* where the ark came to rest as the water subsided, is 17,000 feet high. If this range of mountains was covered, the water was over three miles deep.

One question is, If the water covered the entire earth, where did

---

* Higher Criticism has branded the whole story of Noah and his ark as pure fable. However, since 1856, when a team of scientists with inclinations toward atheism sighted "the remains of Noah's ship," a dozen discoveries on Ararat have been reported. In every instance, the evidence has been lost or destroyed.

Circumstances surrounding more recent efforts to locate the ark make one wonder if God is ready to allow this greatest archaeological find in history. The discovery seems to elude every probe into the frozen wastes of Ararat. Turkish government regulations, unpredictable weather conditions, illness, near-fatal accidents, and shifting snow and ice offer serious obstacles to success.

However, each expedition brings new and exciting facts to light and narrows the focus of the search. Perhaps God will permit full discovery of Noah's ark in the last days as a clear reminder of the judgment of the Lord upon wickedness. Such irrefutable evidence for the Flood could have a direct bearing on modern man's reaction to the scriptural warning about the coming of Christ and the end of the present world order.

it go after the Flood ended? A part of it would have gone back into its underground caverns. The mountains may have pushed up by the awful upheaval, creating deeper basins for the waters. And the *wind* which God caused to "blow over the earth" helped to evaporate great quantities of moisture, returning it to the heavens above the *firmament*. In poetic style, the Hebrew writer expresses it beautifully: "the fountains also of the deep and the windows of heaven were stopped" (8:2).

Noah and the animals were shut up in the ark for approximately a year. The use of a dove was an ingenious way for Noah to determine whether there was any land above water. In such a situation one is forced to live by his wits. When the dove was sent out the second time, it reappeared at the window of the ark, with a leaf in its mouth—a sure sign that it had found land. The third time, when the dove did not return at all, probably having found a home, it was obvious that soon the inhabitants of the ark would be permitted to disembark. But in perfect obedience to Him who had sent him into the ark, Noah waited patiently to make his exodus when the Lord gave permission.

A Covenant with the Earth (8:20—9:29)

In fear and gratitude Noah performed his first act of worship as soon as his feet stood on the drying land. He built an altar, the first specifically mentioned (though not necessarily the first, since Cain and Abel had earlier made sacrifice). On this crude altar, Noah sacrificed one or a pair of each clean bird and animal as a *burnt offering.*

The sweet smell which arose to God has always been a symbol of prayer. As the offering was presented, the commitment made, and the prayer offered, the Lord said that the earth would not again be cursed because of man's sin. Neither would living creatures be punished for man's evil. As long as the earth should last, there would never again be a disturbance of the seasons as had taken place during the year-long Flood. And the reason given for this was the same reason given earlier for the severe judgment: "the imagination of man's heart is evil from his youth" (8:21, see also 6:5). This would imply that while man's sin is ground for destruction, it is also reason for mercy.

The command to be fruitful and populate the earth was again given by the Creator—this time to Noah and his sons. The powers of dominance over the whole creation were once again confirmed. But something new was added. This time God sanctioned the eating of flesh, as He had formerly authorized the eating of plant life (see 9:3). Man had been a vegetarian. Now he could eat flesh, but only under certain specified conditions. No flesh was to be eaten until the blood had been drained from it. The life was in the blood, and that life belonged to the Creator, not to any of His creatures.

Man's blood must not be shed at all, since he is in God's likeness. To kill a man is to seek to deface the divine image itself. No more would Cain's sin and Lamech's irreverence for human life be tolerated by either God or man. Man himself would now be responsible for the punishment of anyone who murdered another person. The treatment was to be in kind—thus we have here the first reference to capital punishment.

The Lord is portrayed as a covenant God throughout the Old and New Testaments. He enters into covenants with Noah, Abraham, the nation of Israel, and the Church. At times the covenants were conditional, at least in their outward benefits; at other times they were unconditional. The covenant with Noah seems definitely to be unconditional. Whatever man might do in the future, the Creator assured him there would never be another flood which would destroy the earth's inhabitants. Before Noah moved back from the altar on which he had offered his sacrifices to the Lord, the promise came to him that there need be no fear of the coming of clouds and rain.

To give a perpetual reminder of this covenant, God created the rainbow (or gave to it a meaning which would henceforth be understood as a sign) to allay man's fear. Peter says that the next time the world is destroyed it will be by fire (2 Peter 3:5-7). The colors of the rainbow have been traditionally understood to represent fire itself.

Noah's three sons have been referred to earlier as inhabitants of the ark with their father. At this point, and not before, we begin to learn something about them. The obvious is mentioned at once —these three sons were to become the fathers of the post-Flood population. Who else could have possibly been appointed?

Immediately, however, we discover that there is a weak link in the family. It is brought to light by a failing of Noah himself and, therefore, cannot be said to have been wholly the fault of the son.

It is affirmed that "Noah was the first tiller of the soil," the first *after the Flood.* Already we have learned that Cain was a farmer who offered the produce from his labors to the Lord. Perhaps this was a new endeavor for Noah (was he a carpenter prior to the Flood?). He did not seem to know how to cope with the powers in the fruit of the vine which he had grown. Drinking to excess, possibly as a kind of happy celebration in which he "toasted" the new age, Noah became incoherently drunk and sprawled nude on the floor of his tent.

The first personal, family, social, and international problem to confront the post-Flood world was caused by intoxicating drink. And drink has been with us continually as a cause of every imaginable form of wickedness since.

After the sin of the first man in the old world, Adam, nakedness was noticed. Now the first man in the new world commits a sin related to nakedness. Exactly what it means we cannot be certain. There is no suggestion that there is anything wrong with the nude form of man *per se.* This is the way the Creator made us and it was *very good.* Nevertheless, once man had involved himself in the experiential wisdom of both good and evil, he immediately acquired the potential for desecrating what was good. No area of human existence lends itself more readily to an abuse of God's good creation than the erotic obsession with the human body. It is an area of great caution for the man or woman who desires to respect "the image of God."

From all appearance, Ham discovered his father's exposed body and reported it to his brothers, Shem and Japheth. There may be a suggestion of homosexual tendencies on the part of Ham— something which would have been totally at odds with the Creator's design for sexual relationships.

On the other hand, the instance may have been nothing more than an attitude of levity and disrespect for the human body. That which sheltered within it the *likeness* of God Himself became a thing of casual laughter. Ham's brothers were more sensitive to the explosive situation and covered their father's body in modest precaution rather than share in the attitude of their irreverent brother. When he awoke from his stupor, Noah learned what had happened and proceeded to place a curse upon Canaan, Ham's son.

Why Ham's son, rather than Ham? The text says that Noah "knew what his younger son had done" (v. 24), which may refer to Canaan rather than Ham. Ham's name always appears second among Noah's three sons, suggesting he was the middle brother, not the youngest. No problem exists in the use of *son* to refer to a grandson, as this was a patriarchal practice. If this assumption is correct, then details of the story are either lost or omitted which would inform us about Canaan's sin. On this view, the responsibility rested on Canaan more than on Ham. It is possible that young Canaan could have been involved in homosexuality.

In patriarchal manner, Noah gave his blessing to his other two sons. The blessings on Shem and Japheth, as well as the curse of Canaan, may have ben normal prophetic observations about the inevitable development of such behavior. Or they could have been angry invective on the part of an embarrassed and hurt father.

The curse on Canaan was that of slavery to his brothers (and two uncles). It may be reasonably assumed that his descendants were also included as slaves to the descendants of others. Shem, being the first-born, was blessed with the personal name of the Lord (*Jahweh Elohim* or Lord God) while Japheth was blessed in the generic divine name only (*Elohim* or God). This reflects the favoritism toward the eldest son—an accepted relationship in oldest times. Japheth and his descendants were "to dwell in the tents of Shem," which may mean that the two would cooperate in their endeavors but that Shem would be considered the superior.

5
THE CREATION
OF THE NATIONS

Genesis 10:1—11:32

Shem, Ham, and Japheth were to become the progenitors of the whole human race. All peoples in the world today find their common ancestry in one of these ancient fathers. This confirms the belief that we are all related by flesh, descending from Noah.

Some general geographical locations can be determined for the three main streams of human history, but nothing precise can be argued since there was much intermarriage across tribal and cultural lines. This accounts for the repetition of names which were sometimes given to individuals and sometimes to entire groups.

The charting of offspring begins with the youngest son, Japheth, who seems to have been the father of the Caucasians of Europe and Asia. Ham was the father of the Egyptians, the pre-Hebrew inhabitants of Palestine, and the Babylonians. Shem stayed in the Mesopotamian valley and became the father of the Semites.

Land and Lineage (10:1-32)
Hardly any of the places named are called by the same terms today. For this reason it is impossible to locate some of them. Others can only be deduced with an educated guess. But there are enough place names which have been discovered to guide us in arriving at geographical areas with rather fluid boundaries. Japheth's descendants lived in the lands north of the cradle of civilization in the Tigris-Euphrates valley. *Gomer* lived in the Crimean area, *Madai* was ancestor to the Medes, *Magog* was far north, *Javan* was

Greece, *Tubal* and *Meschech* were settled near the Black Sea, *Tiras* was father to the Thracians, *Ashkenaz* was in Scythia, *Riphath* was possibly also on the Black Sea.

Togarmah may have been Armenia, *Elishah* was Cyprus, *Tarshish* was in Spain, *Kittim* was the islands of the eastern Mediterranean, *Dodanium* (*Rodanim*) was the island of Rhodes. Some of the above are far less certain than others.

The sons of Ham settled south of the cradle of civilization and are generally located as follows: *Cush,* Ethiopia; *Egypt* needs no clarification since *Mizraim* (translated Egypt) is the Hebrew name for that land; *Put,* east Africa; *Canaan,* Palestine; *Seba, Havilah, Sabtah, Raamah, Sabteca, Sheba,* and *Dedan* were in the south central Arabian country and the African coastland along the Red Sea. All the persons and places listed in verses 13 and 14 are related to Egyptian tribal groups, one of which produced the Philistines.

Canaan (the cursed son of Ham) is given a separate listing. The name refers to tribal groups displaced by the Hebrews under Joshua plus some other tribes which migrated as far north as Asia Minor.

This is a good place to correct an erroneous and tragic tradition which has circulated widely. It has been argued that the black race was cursed by God when Ham sinned and that the people of the Negroid community are destined to remain in slavery or servitude. Such a theory is the creation of racially prejudiced minds seeking proof texts for unchristian attitudes, or just the result of a tradition of ignorance.

Clearly it is recorded that Ham's descendants formed what we know today as the black peoples of the world.*

However, it was not Ham who was cursed, but his son Canaan, whose descendants were the people of Palestine. They cannot by any stretch of the imagination be anthropologically classified as Negroid!

An entire section (10:15-19) is given to Canaan's offspring, showing they were separated from the other sons of Ham who

---

* The word *Ham* means "black" or "dark." Most likely, the dark skin color was by design of God in preparation for the dispersion of nations soon to take place. Black people are not dark because they lived in the hot suns of Africa. Rather they migrated to that area because their pigmented skin made them more comfortable in the sun-baked world. Lighter skinned peoples, who descended from Japheth, naturally sought out more temperate climates. The olive-skinned sons of Shem were able to adjust rather well to either type of climatic conditions.

were black peoples.* Let it be stated emphatically that the tradition which makes the Negro the descendant of Canaan and, therefore, a slave, is without support. Frankly, there is no way to distinguish the three lines of descent from Noah with any dogmatism due to millennia of crossbreeding.

The sons of Shem lived mainly in the center of the spreading nations in the area of civilization's birth. *Eber* was the father of the Hebrews and the line through which Christ was later to be born (Luke 3:35). *Elam* lay east of Babylon, *Asshur* was father to the Assyrians, *Arpachshad* was possibly northeast of Nineveh, *Lud* may have been Lydia, *Aram* was Syria, *Uz* may have lain in the Syrian desert, *Hul* was possibly in west Syria, *Gether* and *Mash* are totally unknown, and *Joktan* was a multiplicity of tribes in Arabia. We cannot go beyond this with any degree of certainty. In fact, even some of the above is foggy!

The important thing to observe is that the populace of the ancient world spread to the north and south of the garden of Eden and eventually covered the whole known world.

One additional observation may be made in relation to one named *Peleg* who lived in days when "the earth was divided" (10:25). This reference is probably to the division of the nations described in the story of the Tower of Babel.

Let us return now for a moment to the lineage of Ham, in which is given an interesting bit of information about a particular descendant named *Nimrod*. This son of Ham is called a "mighty man" and "a mighty hunter." Because of his prowess as a great hunter of animals (and possibly warrior among men) he was highly respected and feared by his peers. Thus he automatically was thrust into a position of leadership and was made the earth's first king. We know this to be true because Scripture mentions his *kingdom* as "Babel, and Erech, and Accad, and Calneh in the land of Shinar" (10:9-10).

The inserted story of Nimrod is a prelude to what happened after the confusion of the nations at the Tower of Babel. Nimrod built a mighty kingdom at Babylon, spreading his power to include neighboring areas, finally establishing his confederacy as far away as Nineveh. He was the great builder of cities, continuing what Cain had begun, in an effort to make man adequate without de-

---

* For an understanding of this variation of skin pigmentation in the same family, one should familiarize himself with the genetic principles laid down in Mendel's Laws.

pendence upon God. The confederation of city life deceptively offered man power and security in industry, economics, and military defenses. He should have sought security in the Lord Himself!

It was at this time in the ancient world that colonialism was born, and the struggle for control of kingdoms began. Babylon remained the leading power after the Babel episode until replaced by other descendants of Ham who founded the powerful Egyptian kingdom.

The Confusion of Tongues (11:1-9)

Many towers were built in the ancient world—maybe they were forerunners of the pyramids—but the Tower of Babel was the first. And it was unfinished, due to a rather strange interruption. Descendants of Noah, who had begun to multiply in obedience to the Lord's command, gradually began their migration back from the eastern mountains where the ark rested. They came to the Mesopotamian valley of their ancestors.

As is so often the case with Hebrew history, the account of this migration is an amplification of the generalities in the previous story of the three lines of descent. This indicates that the event now being described took place prior to the dispersion of the peoples of Shem, Ham, and Japheth listed in the foregoing chapter. It was the problem at the new construction site in the plains of Shinar which scattered the people across the earth. The author backtracks now to explain what caused this unusual dispersion. The whole thing started with a gigantic homecoming of the children of Noah.

At the time of the migration from Ararat and the surrounding mountains, all the people spoke a single language. Articulate communication was very simple. It was not cluttered with complex peculiarities characteristic of most languages and dialects today.

Obedience to the Lord's command to fill the earth required a scattering into all the world. Maybe for protection or the continuance of family solidarity, the people decided to get together and build a city. In so doing, the plan of God was apt to be defeated. The land of Shinar, around what historians know as Babylon, was the place where they settled down to burn bricks and build their dream city.

It was all a purely selfish pursuit as they wanted "to make a name" for themselves which would bind them together, rather than be scattered. Their whole mistake lay in the fact that they were not including the Creator in their plans. They were attempting to unify the human race by purely manmade blueprints.

Perhaps in the wall of their city, the people planned to build a tower. Watchtowers were not uncommon in later cites where walls were erected for security. But this tower was to have "its top in the heavens." Succeeding towers, called *Ziggurats,* had pagan temples constructed on their summits, but this earliest edifice was not so advanced.

The purpose was not to honor a particular deity, but to glorify themselves. They were going to be their own god! These descendants of Noah probably had no faith in the Creator's rainbow sign. With the story of the great Flood still in their minds, they were perhaps seeking to outdo the Eternal by building a tower which would save them from the next deluge. It was all a symbol of their self-sufficiency, their independence from "the tyranny of a sovereign God."

Still the devil was seducing men to be *like God* by trying to outsmart Him.

In anthropomorphic terms, God is said to have come down to see what these people were attempting. Having seen their elaborate building program and been fully aware of what they were planning to do with it, the Godhead was again called into divine session. A decision was reached as to what had to be done. Since the tower was "only a beginning" of what would eventually be accomplished by a united sinful race, the Lord set about to break up man's smug little plan of rebellion.

All that was needed was for the Creator, who had given man his power to communicate (a facet of the *likeness* of God), to withdraw just enough of that power to make man's vocalizing little better than the sounds emitted from the mouths of the beasts and the fowl. When they could not understand each other, further work on the tower became virtually impossible. Even if the task could have been completed, life together would have been unthinkable!

Completely frustrated by the intolerable situation, the throngs of workmen suddenly packed up their belongings and "left off building the city." From Babylon, called *Babel* at this early date, the masses of people scattered in all directions. We have already reported the areas of the world in which they finally settled. In this way, the original plan of God to fill the earth was realized.

One of the outstanding motifs in the running Bible account from Genesis to Revelation is the established fact that *the Creator will not be defeated in His original design for His world.* Confusion was only a temporary arrangement necessary to accomplish the divine purpose at that moment in time. God would eventually restore order out of the confusion of tongues. Zephaniah prophesied of that day when he wrote, "At that time I will change the speech of the peoples to a pure speech" (Zeph. 3:9, LB, footnote), that all of them may call on the name of the Lord and serve Him with one accord. On the Day of Pentecost it happened. Men from all parts of the world heard the divine Word through the disciples, "every man in our own tongue" (Acts 2:8). All present understood. In some divine manner, God had reversed the confusion created by man's sin with the order created by the Holy Spirit.

Order Out Of Confusion (11:10-32)

Genealogical accounts can be tiresome unless they trace one's own ancestral history. Even then they often become tedious and uninteresting due to missing links in almost all such family records. This is now the third time in the Genesis story when we have come upon a genealogy. The first was Seth's, the second Noah's, and now Shem's. Already we have observed how interesting these family trees can be when studied carefully. Many of these persons were named in the previous chapter. One thing stands out, however, in that the genealogical record of Shem's offspring ends with a perfectly smooth transition into the family of Terah. Terah was a Semite who was a practicing pagan, but who was destined to give to the world one of its most renowned sons.

Terah lived with his wife, three sons, two daughters-in-law, a grandson, and possibly several other relatives. They dwelt in Ur of the Chaldees, one of the thriving cities which grew up as a result of the scattering of peoples after the failure at Babel.

Ur was a cultural center, immensely wealthy. Located on the Euphrates River not far from the Persian Gulf, the city boasted a strong commercial superiority. The culture was graced with an advanced degree of crafts, an educational system of much repute, and a religious complex which included a temple to Nannar, the Moongod, and Ningal, the Moon-goddess. Terah worshiped these deities and led his family in such practice.

The middle class in Ur enjoyed unbelievable luxury for a period in history which preceded the birth of Christ by over 2,000 years. Scholars have excavated houses which belonged to middle-class people and report that they contained as many as 20 rooms—hardly ever less than 10! Terah may have lived in this kind of house with his family, one of whom was named *Abram.*

All of this implies that Abram had everything he wanted in a wealthy and aggressive city.

Then, Abram's brother Haran suddenly died. Terah was so broken by what happened that the good things of life seemed to lose their luster and attraction. It was suggested that the family all move away. Perhaps the change would help them forget the grief which was accented by every familiar thing which Haran had touched. So four of them—Terah, Abram, his wife Sarai, and Haran's son, Lot—began a pilgrimage into the north country. Since no further reference is made to Abram's brother Nahor and his family, we may assume they chose to remain in Ur.

The destination planned by Terah was the distant land of Canaan, the home of the peoples of the cursed son of Ham. But they stopped at Haran, which may have been later named for Terah's deceased son. There Abram buried his father, who died at the age of 205.

Since Egypt will be figuring largely in future events in the biblical narrative, it is well for us to note here that the Mesopotamian valley was not the only part of the world making tremendous strides developing culture. Babylon was a powerful kingdom under the rule of Amraphel (Gen. 14:1), who was king during the time of Abram. But the Old Kingdom in Egypt had possibly been in existence since the time of Nimrod. The pyramids were built nearly 500 years before Abram's day. During the Middle Kingdom, about the time of Abram, Egypt was experiencing great prosperity. Ham's descendants had done a phenomenal thing in creating a powerful succession of dynasties which were soon to steal the ancient world's glory from the Babylonian empire. In less than 300 years, the people of the world would be at the mercy of the pharaoh, who with his Hebrew governor, Joseph, would be dispensing grain to a famine-starved world.

6
THE DIVINE
CHOICE

Genesis 12:1—20:18

According to Stephen, the call of Abram came while he was still in Ur (Acts 7:2). In fact, Abram may have felt an urge to wander before he really understood the reason. On the other hand, he could have heard the call of the unknown Deity and shared it with his father, Terah, who may have been quite ready to leave the place of his haunting memories.

Speculation answers no questions, so we drop the matter there. What is clear in the Scriptures is that God distinctly called Abram upon the occasion of his father's death in Haran. Often in times of prolonged illness and the eventual death of a loved one, the sense of the supernatural is keener. God sometimes has His best chance to speak to us when our hearts ache with loneliness.

The Call at Haran (12:1-9)

Abram had left his country, his kindred, and his father's house. At Haran the Lord God made it perfectly clear to him that he was not to return to Ur of the Chaldees. To leave all that has surrounded one with a sense of communal and family ties is never easy. But what made this exceptional was Abram's total ignorance as to where he was going, and his uncertainty about the identity of the divine voice which was challenging him. No assurance was given to him except that this *new* God would lead him into a new land which would be easily recognized. For his obedience, God promised a sizeable reward—divine favor, many descendants, world renown, protection, and the satisfaction of having made an eternal contribution to the life of the world. Who could wish for more?

Centuries have passed since that day in Haran, and all those promises either have been fulfilled or are in the process of being fulfilled now. There is no question about Abram's greatness. Not only do the Jews honor him, but Christians and Muslims as well include him in their roster of holy men. And his greatness lies in his unquestioning obedience to the call. Acting with his household, which included his nephew and all the servants acquired in Haran, he began the adventure of the ages.

Like Noah before him, Abram built an altar upon his arrival in the land of Canaan (12:7). His first stop was at Shechem, located in the geographical center of the country. About 700 years later, Joshua claimed the land of Canaan for the Hebrews at this exact spot. He may have paused there because of the incomparable beauty of the famous pass between the mountains of Ebal and Gerizim where the Samaritans much later were to build their rival temple. The *terebinth* (usually translated as *oak tree* but more likely some kind of evergreen) which stood there was probably the most impressive in the area because it had been chosen as a sacred tree by the inhabitants of Canaan.

It's not unreasonable to suppose that a sage, in whom it was believed "dwelt the spirit of the gods," had set up his oracular offices there. *Moreh* may have this meaning. If this is true, then Abram probably talked with the holy man of the pagan culture until God appeared to him saying, "Unto thy seed will I give this land" (12:7). The Lord was warning against taking counsel from wise pagan sages and, at the same time, revealing the secret thus far hidden from Abram. Canaan was to be the place where the divine Creator would begin His work of redeeming the fallen race. It was to begin with Abram of Ur and be completed with Jesus of Nazareth.

No information is given us as to how Abram happened to know of *Jahweh Elohim,* the Lord God. Maybe Abram did not know about the true Lord at all until He revealed Himself to Abram, much as He would manifest Himself in the future to Moses in the uncovering of the mysteries of creation. But maybe he did know something about this God of Shem, his famous ancestor. Noah was possibly still living and keeping the story of the Flood alive in the midst of growing idolatry. That Abram may have been intrigued by the ancient story more than by the moon-god and goddess of Ur is not incredible. Perhaps he was then searching for some living contact with that God whom his forefathers claimed to have made the world and spoken personally to old Noah.

If all that is true, when the Lord called to him, Abram was ready to follow. And when that same voice confirmed the promise of faith at Shechem, he built an altar and worshipped. Everywhere Abram went he announced to the Canaanites his faith in the one true God. As at Shechem, so at Bethel and Hebron he would build altars.

Abram's Struggle for Survival (12:10—17:14)
Abram's deception (12:10-20)

Man is always man, even when he walks with God. His depraved nature keeps coming to the surface in spite of everything.

No one except Christ Himself has ever been free from the nature of the first Adam. Jesus Christ was the second Adam, the beginning of a new humanity, and He knew no sin. Faith in His redemptive work and obedience to His words of life can give us final victory over the Adamic curse, but so long as we live in the world there is no *eradication* of our old nature. And if we think that we have problems with the carnality of our existence, imagine what Abram must have had to contend with before the coming of the Saviour!

Before Abram had been in Canaan more than a short time, famine threatened the people. Famines were not unusual among the "servant" Canaanites, who had learned to handle the problem without panic. But Abram was different. His background was one of plenty so he knew nothing about the pinching pains of hunger. The land of Egypt, watered as it was by the canals from the Nile (they had been built in Abram's time and were the talk of the ancient world), was never lacking for food. Therefore, without waiting for the guidance of the Lord and failing to trust Him who had brought him this far, Abram set out to relieve his fear of starvation. He went to the strange world of the ancient Hamites.

Customs among the Egyptians were somewhat different than those Abram was used to in Ur, and he knew it. Kings and princes had a way of stealing women whom they considered beautiful. If the women were married, there was really no problem—they just murdered the husbands! Ancient documents, as well as traditions, show this. Therefore, Abram decided to guard against being killed.

His plans were not very thoughtful toward Sarai, his beautiful wife, though they were clever. When they crossed the border he insisted that Sarai tell the Egyptians she was Abram's *sister* lest he be killed on the spot. It's hard to conceive of any man's being so free with his wife as to save his own life by inviting the violation of her body. But *all* customs were different then, and the wife did as she was told!

Sure enough, it happened as he suspected it would. When they beheld her physical beauty, the Egyptians informed Pharaoh of this jewel which ought to be added to his harem. At once Sarai was summoned and, as a dowry, Pharaoh lavished upon her "brother" (Abram *was* her half-brother) servants and cattle in abundance.

But soon it did not go well with the king of Egypt because what had taken place was not right. If unchecked, the deplorable situation could destroy the Lord's ultimate plan of redemption. Sarai was to be the maternal ancestor of the Son of God—she must not be defiled by Pharaoh.

It would appear to us that God should have punished Abram instead of Pharaoh—and perhaps Abram's later struggles were disciplinary—but that would not have gotten Sarai back. When the plagues fell on the royal household, the king knew something was wrong and immediately realized the stranger's deceit. Normally such a man would have been put to death, but God was in this picture. Pharaoh was so afraid that he sent Sarai back to Abram and issued an ultimatum that they get out of Egypt. The plagues foreshadowed what was to happen to another Pharaoh who would hold other Hebrews as his captives. God had promised protection, and He would not deny His word.

Abram and Lot Separate (13:1-18)

With the riches brought with them from Ur and the additional wealth given to Abram and Sarai by Pharaoh, this fortunate couple and their nephew, Lot, retraced their steps to Canaan. They crossed the Negeb, a hot, barren, dry desert land southwest of the Dead Sea, where only nomads could survive. Their pilgrimage carried them back to Bethel, 10 miles north of Jerusalem in the hill country. There Abram had built an altar on his travels south. Now he again offered worship to Jehovah, probably at that same altar (13:4).

No sooner had Abram come from worship than he was confronted with a serious problem that was precipitated by the extreme wealth of both Lot and himself. The two men's herds and flocks had multiplied so rapidly that the grazing area was not big enough to supply grass for them all. It's quite likely that Abram did not relish the idea of being separated from Lot in a strange and alien land. But quarreling between the herdsmen of the cattle and the shepherds of the sheep might eventually create friction between the uncle and nephew themselves. The problem was one which had to be taken care of at once.

Though "the Canaanite and Perizzite dwelled then in the land" (the origin of Perizzites is unknown but they were some sub-grouping of Canaan's offspring), the land was still not densely populated, especially in the Jordanian hill country. The two newcomers could find "squatters rights." Therefore, standing at Bethel, one of the highest points in Palestine, the two men scanned the surrounding countryside. Magnanimous spirit that he was, the older man, Abram, gave first choice to his nephew. He offered him either the pasture land to the east or west ("left or right" may mean north or south instead since we do not know which way they were facing). When Lot saw the plains of Sodom (which were at the *south* edge of the Dead Sea) and the ·Jordan valley (which was east), and realized that they were well-watered and quite fertile, he chose to dwell in the valleys with his flocks. Evidence made possible by scientific digging shows that Lot chose an area which, at that early time, was luxuriant with growth.

But alas, a good place to raise cattle is not always a good place to rear children. The people of Sodom were "wicked and sinners before the Lord" (13:13).

When Lot had gathered his tents, wealth, and servants together he departed for his new and promising residence. At last God and Abram were alone. Then the Lord instructed Abram to look around him in every direction, to rise and walk through the whole land. Everything as far as he could see would be given to him and his offspring.

The covenant was unconditional and eternally binding. The children of Abram were guaranteed the land of Canaan as a possession *forever.*

Today, after hundreds of years of wanderings and persecutions, the sons of Abram are back in the land of promise. And from it they shall never again depart! The biblical prophecies of the great return are now being brought to pass before our eyes with amazing rapidity.

With the promise ringing in his ears, Abram arose and traveled south where he dwelt by the *terebinths* (oak trees or evergreens) of Mamre (another name for Hebron). There he renewed his faith and declared his allegiance to the Lord by building another altar at this *high place* where pagan altars may have already stood.

Abram fights for his nephew (14:1-24)

The international character of chapter 14 makes it a unique part of the Genesis account. Some have argued that it is a complete story written totally outside the biblical narrative and inserted at this point. It is further argued from this supposition that this story was added to lend credence to the historicity of Abram and portray him as a world figure in the thought of pagan writers.

Such a theory is not necessary at all. True, the whole chapter has certain distinguishable characteristics which set it off from the rest of the book. No restrictions should be placed upon Moses, however, in his ability to tell a particular story in a manner unique from the rest of the book. The content of this chapter deals with a wider world of activity—that may account for its having been told in a different manner. If one does not rule out the divine inspiration of Moses, he has no problem at this point. The chapter is strategically important from an historical point of view and the earlier surmise that it is legendary has been disproved.

A summary of the events described in this chapter will be helpful in view of the names of strange kings and places. At some earlier time the five kings whose realms lay in the fertile area to the south of the Dead Sea (where Lot was now living) had been under the enforced dominance of Chedorlaomer, king of Elam, which lay to the east of Shinar. After 12 years of this foreign dominance, the kings in the valley of the Dead Sea (here called Valley of Siddim) formed a confederacy and revolted. About a year afterward, four kings from Mesopotamia came with their armed men and entered into battle with the five kings of the plains on the shores of the Dead Sea. Other cities were conquered and plundered as well. The power of the enemy was so great that the kings of the plains ran for their lives, some falling into the slime pits which surrounded the sea. When the "smoke of battle" cleared, the Mesopotamian kings had taken everything from the valley, including Lot, his family, and his wealth.

When Abram was informed of the massacre and the capture of Lot, he was incensed at the audacity which would incite men of royal power to take advantage of an innocent herdsman who wanted to live in peace. Immediately Abram prepared a hot pursuit of the wicked kings from his old homeland. The Scripture indicates that he had found some friends near Hebron who were willing to go with him, probably with the agreement that he would defend them if they should run into such an emergency at some future date. The 318 "trained men, born in his house" (14:14) were leaders for the battle. Perhaps there were several hundreds or even thousands of armed men who accompanied the leading officers.

At Dan, in the far north of upper Canaan, about 50 miles from Damascus, Abram worked out his strategy and attacked the enemy. Beyond Damascus he pursued the routed forces of Chedorlaomer, retrieved the goods which had been stolen from the five kings in the valley, and brought back Lot with his family and possessions.

When Abram returned to the plains, Bera, the king of Sodom, met him. King Bera offered Abram all the wealth he had retrieved as a reward for the return of the captives. But Abram rejected the reward on the grounds that God was his provider and he had utmost faith in the Lord. Furthermore, Abram could not afford to be enriched by a pagan king. In the days ahead when the descendants of Abram would make conquest of the land, there must be no obligation to anyone in the area—only to God! He did suggest that his pagan allies be given their share of the spoils since this would not complicate his own relationship with the covenant God.

A second king was also present at this meeting with the Hebrew patriarch. He was named *Melchizedek,* and he was the king of Salem, which is unquestionably the city of Jerusalem. With the bread and wine which he had brought to Abram, he also gave his blessing, for he was a "priest of God Most High." The blessing which he gave to Abram indicates that he too was a worshiper of Jehovah. He spoke of God as "maker of heaven and earth," which may reflect a genuine reverence for the Creator who spoke with Adam, Enoch, and Noah before him. Melchizedek was sure that the same God who created the universe had also delivered the enemies into the hand of the Hebrew patriarch. There were not many gods, each doing some specific thing, but one God who did it all!

Abram recognized this priest-king who was already in Canaan before Abram came to dwell there. It was as if the Lord had placed His holy man there to await the arrival of the father of a people whom the "Most High God" had chosen. So Abram the conquering warrior gave tithes of all he had to this priest, an acknowledgment of the right of Melchizedek to represent the Lord and of the debt which every man owes the Lord God.

Who was Melchizedek? No one knows with any certainty. He is shrouded in mystery. Nothing in history even hints at his genealogy. We do not know his father or his mother. Apparently his beginning and ending are deliberately obscured; his kingly priesthood was never meant to be a part of the earthly order of Aaron. Thus he has come to be a type of the Messiah who is "a priest forever after the order of Melchizedek" (Ps. 110:4).

The letter to the Hebrews points out the similarities between Melchizedek and the Messiah (Heb. 6:19—7:17): they were both above Abram, outside the tribe of Levi, of unknown beginning and ending, and kings as well as priests. Christ's ministry was and is kingly and priestly. And the day will finally come in the Millennium when the returned Redeemer will "rule upon His throne and He shall be a priest upon His throne: and the counsel of peace shall be between them both" (Zech. 6:13). Thus we have in this ancient account a sign and foretype of the coming of the Messiah and His earthly reign.

First renewal of the Covenant (15:1—16:16)

This is the first time we have been told of a vision. God has communicated with men, but the author has not told us how. It is not possible to tell whether this new word implies that all preceding dialogues between God and man were in visions. This could well have been a new approach by the divine Spirit to mortal flesh.

In the vision the Lord reiterated the certainty of protection *(shield)* and posterity *(reward)*. By this time, as we well understand, Abram was needing some encouragement. He had gotten himself in trouble in Egypt, suffered separation from his kinsman, and gotten involved in a bloody war. Things had not gone as smoothly as had been anticipated.

The most perplexing of all the confusing problems to confront Abram was the continued childessness of Sarai. How could God give him a reward in posterity if he was destined to be married to a wife who would remain barren all her days?

Eliezer, a servant from Damascus, had been selected out of all the household to be the heir in the event no child was born to the family. Such a custom was prevalent in that day. In exchange for the inheritance the servant agreed to care for the masters until they were dead and properly buried. A contract had been discussed which would make Eliezer legal heir to Abram's wealth and name. Was the Lord going to let a thing like that happen after specifically guaranteeing the Hebrew patriarch a son?

The Lord God spoke emphatically in confirmation of the original promise: "This man will not be your heir, but one who shall come forth from your own body, he shall be your heir" (15:4, NASB). Pointing him to the stars, the number of which was beyond his powers to determine, God assured Abram that he would have as many descendants as there were stars in those skies.

And the Scripture says that Abram believed.

That was not the easiest thing to do, considering that God had made a lot of promises about numerous seed but had not yet produced one! But it was because he believed in spite of the way things looked to him that the Lord "counted it to him for righteousness" (15:6).

For the first time in the redemptive plan of God we have come upon the initial divine explanation of the way in which man was to be redeemed: *by faith alone.*

Abram had already made a lot of tragic mistakes and he would make many more, but that was not the important thing. The thing that really counted was whether he would believe what God had said and trust His promise. And that is the note which is struck again and again throughout the rest of the Bible, especially in the New Testament. As Abram believed God's promise, so we must believe in Him who came to redeem us—Jesus Christ. We must take Him at His word, letting our full weight down upon the atoning blood of Jesus Christ. Paul goes to great lengths to compare Abram's saving faith to that of the Christain under grace (Rom. 4:3, 9, 22-24; Gal. 3:6). And the writer to the Hebrews clearly rests the entire journey and achievements of the patriarch upon his faith (Heb. 11:8-19).

To visibly ratify the covenant between them, the Lord demanded a strange kind of sacrifice—strange to us at least—but not unusual for the time. A heifer, she-goat, and ram were cut in half and placed over against each other (15:9-10). The turtledove and pigeon which Abram brought to the scene were not slain at all. In keeping with cultic practices, which were adapted for their own symbolic purposes in ancient Israel, the two halves represented the two parties of the covenant. As Abram fell into a sleep (just at the approach of twilight), he was possessed with a sense of fear. Everything became ominously dark, and the Lord told him what would befall his people in days to come. Nothing was withheld from him. The 400 years of Egyptian slavery were predicted, but a promise of punishment for the oppressors and great reward for the oppressed was given. Abram's aged and peaceful death was mentioned as was the return of the Hebrews from slavery *in the fourth generation* (probably fourth cycle of time).

The reference to the Amorites' iniquity having not yet been completed was simply God's way of saying that the time was not ripe for conquest of Canaan. *Amorites* was a collective name often used for the populace of Canaan prior to Joshua's time.

It must have been an eerie sight which Abram beheld in the darkness of the night and the melancholy of his soul. God appeared in the symbol of fire and smoke (as He later would to Moses at Sinai), referred to here as a "smoking oven and a flaming torch" (15:17, NASB). The pot (or oven) and the torch passed between the cut halves of the animals as God reaffirmed the covenant, adding some specifics. Customarily, both parties of a covenant would pass between the symbolic halves. In this way each one swore to keep his share of the agreement under penalty of suffering the same fate which had come to the animals. Sometimes only the weaker party made the walk.

In this case Abram did not walk between the halves—only God. The Lord was putting His own honor and integrity on the line for a mortal being—an act not unlike when the Son of God became poor that we might become rich.

When the birds, which had not been cut in half, came down upon the covenant-pieces, Abram drove them away. This was symbolic of the determination of both God and man that nothing should interfere with the agreement.

Boundaries for the new people were clearly stated in the specifics of the ratified covenant. The "river of Egypt" was at the border of Egypt and was more like a wadi or gully than a river.

It was near the southwest extremity of Canaan. The Euphrates River ran at the edge of the northeast border of Solomon's kingdom near a city called *Tiphsah.*

Ten tribal groups of the peoples who inhabited the land in the age of the patriarchs are mentioned as being finally expelled to make way for the Hebrews. Kenites and Kenizzites were clans who lived in the extreme south (Negeb) desert and were to be taken over by the Hebrew tribe of Judah.

With incredible accuracy the future of the kingdom of Israel was predicted nearly 700 years before Joshua returned from Egypt to bring it to pass. It is all an irrefutable proof that the message as recorded in the Bible is the inspired Word of God.

An attempt to produce an heir (16:1-16)

We have earlier learned that Sarai was barren; she had given birth to no children since her marriage to Terah's son. In line with the custom of the day among many pagan societies, Sarai eventually admitted defeat as a child-bearer and offered her slave girl to produce a child for Abram. The concubine would bear her master's child, which would be delivered with the slave girl across the wife's knees, as an offspring who would be considered a legitimate heir unless Sarai should later conceive. There was nothing out of the ordinary about the procedure. The practice was native to these peoples and explains, in the light of the progressive revelation of the Lord, why concubinage was *allowed* the people of the covenant for many years.

Where the patriarch and his wife did wrong was in being impatient at the very moment when God had reaffirmed the covenant with a symbolic sacrifice. Without question Abram had been guaranteed his own son for an heir. The assurance that his servant would not be his heir should have made it obvious that the heir would not be the child of a slave either. In following pagan customs Abram and Sarai were attempting, as Adam and Eve had, to run their own lives without regard to what God had said. Abram had *believed,* and God had imputed righteousness to him. But now he is listening to Sarai, as Adam hearkened to Eve, rather than to the Lord. Man is always prone to take matters into his own hands when the divine plan appears to be developing too slowly. It is one of mankind's greatest weaknesses!

The unhappy result of this man-made solution to the problem issued in a quarrel between Sarai and Hagar (the Egyptian concubine). This put Abram on the spot. When Hagar discovered that she was pregnant, "she looked with contempt upon her mistress" (16:4, AMP). That is, Sarai's esteem was lowered in Hagar's eyes because she, a slave, had conceived while Sarai had been unable to do so.

Perhaps Hagar even laughed at Sarai and poked fun at her barrenness. It was more than the wife could take. She was embarrassed and humiliated, so she put the responsibility on her husband by insisting that he take care of the matter. From the Code of Hammurabi (an ancient code of ethics from the general area of Abram's birthplace), we learn that such a slave could not elevate herself without being demoted to a lower level of slavery. The slave girl could not be expelled by the mistress. Therefore Abram gave his wife permission to do what was necessary to rectify the embarrassing situation. Sarai, however, abused Hagar so severely that the slave girl left of her own accord. We may be quite safe in assuming that this was Sarai's intent all along.

When the angel of God found Hagar quenching her thirst by a spring in the wilderness, he sent her back to Sarai with the explicit command that she should behave herself and stay in her proper place. With this light reprimand, the angelic messenger also made Hagar a promise, since the covenant with Abraham included all his descendants. He promised that Hagar's son would be the father of a multitude and that he should be named *Ishmael* ("God will hear").

Ishmael's temperament was predicted—he would be "as a wild ass among men" (16:12, AMP), constantly engaged in conflict with his own kinsmen, namely the descendants of the son later to be born to Sarai. It is a known fact that the Ishmaelites caused the Israelites untold trouble in later generations. The Arabic peoples are the descendants of Hagar's son, and, after 4,000 years, are still the Hebrew's bitterest foe.

Mohammed claimed to be descended from Ishmael, and it is prophetic to note that Christianity, a kind of spiritual Israel in prophetic history, has always had a struggle with the Muslim faith. Abram's mistake in impatience and lack of trust in Jehovah created many difficulties for both Jews and Christians for some 4,000 years!

Hagar named the spring where the angel spoke to her *Beer-*

lahairoi (the well of the vision of life). Amazed that she, a slave girl running away from the household of Abram, could *see* God and still live, Hagar memorialized the occasion by naming the place. The experience must have shocked her into reality and frightened her immeasurably. Without delay she returned to Sarai and was apparently faithful and obedient.

At the age of 86, Abram looked for the first time into the face of his slave-heir, Ishmael. Little did he know what trouble the chosen people of God were destined to have because of that innocent-looking babe in the arms of Hagar.

Second renewal of the Covenant (17:1-14)

Over a decade passed before we have record of the Lord God speaking to Abram again. Perhaps the years of divine silence were a discipline meted out to one who had run ahead of his God, to get him to learn the art of waiting. May it not be that the rightful heir would have been born much sooner if his parents had not tried to outdistance the Creator?

When God did finally appear again to Abram, now 99, He warned the impatient patriarch that from henceforth he must recognize Jehovah as *God Almighty (El Shaddai)*. This meant that the Lord of Abram had adequate resources to accomplish what He had promised. It further implied that He would not tolerate any more behavior such as represented by the relationship with Hagar. And to insist on this, Abram was instructed to walk *before* God. Previously Enoch and Noah are said to have walked *with* the Lord. Now things must be altered. Abram must walk *before* the Almighty God where the Lord could keep an eye on him constantly!

With this subtle word of disapproval the God of mercy again reaffirmed the covenant which was still in force. Abram must not forget it.

The main features of the divine covenant were held up: progeny, reward, perpetuity, and national glory. Now the identification of his descendants as *kings* was added (v. 6). This was the first mention of the kingdom of Israel, which figures so prominently in the Old Testament and is actually a thread which ties the entire Bible together. It is that kingdom which shall have no end. Furthermore, the Creator insisted that He "will be their God," a fact which is currently referred to by the contemporary expression, "the God of the Jews."

The change of Abram's name to *Abraham* was indicative of a new start after the failure with Hagar that resulted in 13 years of what saints despairingly refer to as "the silence of God." Abram means "high father" and Abraham means "father of a multitude." There was little difference in the name—as is the case when Sarai's was altered to *Sarah* a little later. It is fairly obvious that the name change meant basically a new start for both Abram and his wife.

At the giving of Abraham's new name, the Lord initiated a sign of the covenant which would forever mark the faithful Hebrew family—circumcision. The custom was not new in the ancient world since Egyptians practiced it as well as the Edomites. Ammonites, and Moabites. It was foreign to the people of Mesopotamia, however, and thus a new point of departure for Abraham who hailed from that part of the world.

Circumcision was to have a unique meaning for the Hebrews. The "cutting off" was a symbol of their being a separate people on whom God had specifically placed His hand. Significantly it was asserted that he who was not "cut off" from the pagan culture about him was automatically to be cut off from the people of God. This did not mean that there would be no interchange of commerce or communication with other peoples. On the contrary, the Hebrews were to be the divine instrument for reaching the nations. But they were to be a people separated (sanctified or set apart) for His purposes.

The time of circumcision was set at precisely eight days of age. Of course, the males who were already older were to be circumcised as a sign of the covenant immediately, regardless of their age.

Walking by Faith (17:15—20:18)
Promise of Isaac's birth (17:15—18:15)
Abraham was 99 and Ishmael was 13 when the bloody surgery was performed. Every slave purchased or born in Abraham's house was forced to endure the painful procedure along with the patriarch and the son of Hagar. But before the actual deed was performed, the Lord emphasized that in no way was Abraham to think that the circumcision of Ishmael meant that he was to be the heir. It was the beginning of a new day and his 99 years would not be a deterrent to the coming of a son.

Though Sarah was 90 years old, she would share in the blessing.

Her name would be changed, her barrenness removed. She would yet bear a son for Abraham who would carry on the covenant entered into by Abraham and the Lord God. The child would be named Isaac (laughter), because both the patriarch and his wife laughed in utter incredulity at the very thought of generating a son at their age. Perhaps the name would be a constant reminder to them of their slowness to believe what God had promised.

It all seemed so unlikely that Abraham dared to suggest to the Lord that Ishmael should be chosen to continue the covenant relationship. The boy was already there and had reached the manly age of 13. He was to be circumcised as the first of the patriarch's seed. Logic would say that he ought to be elected. All this continued talk about a son for Sarah seemed so incredible at her age and even unnecessary. But God rejected man's substitute for the divine plan. He always does.

Ishmael was not to be the elected heir, but he would not be forgotten. Jehovah promised his father that the lad Ishmael would father 12 sons who would become princes of a great nation. They were to become, as we have previously noted, the Arabic peoples, eternally sworn enemies of the Hebrews.

Now that God's plan had been revealed to Abraham, it would need to be given to Sarah. Rather than to trust Abraham with so important a message, the Lord delivered it Himself. And He did it in a strange way. The variety of ways in which the Lord revealed Himself to the patriarchs is an indication of His power and wisdom. Three angelic messengers approached Abraham one day as he sat in the shade of the grove at Mamre (Hebron). One of the angels seems to be the Lord Himself, possibly the preexistent Christ. With the typical graces of an easterner, Abraham arose and welcomed the strangers as guests at his tent. Water was brought for their feet and an offer of bread was made to refresh them (18:4-5). By now it had begun to dawn on the patriarch who the Spokesman of the three actually was. Could it have been the authority in His voice? Or was it something He said? We do not know. All we can be reasonably certain about is that the preparation of the ensuing feast with a roasted calf and all the trimmings was more than would have been done for an ordinary stranger. Something about the angels in human form convinced the startled host that *God Almighty* was at his tent.

It would not be the usual thing for total strangers to ask so soon about the host's wife. The very mention of her name by the divine Spokesman was enough to let Abraham know that the strangers were quite familiar with his household (18:9). Replying that she was in the tent, Abraham heard the announcement of the forthcoming motherhood of Sarah, just as the Lord had spoken to him before.

When Sarah, who was eavesdropping behind the curtain, heard what the guest said, she laughed silently. The idea of her conceiving a child at 90 years of age and becoming a mother in due time was enough to break her up. But the Lord, from whom no secrets are hid and unto whom all desires are known, perceived what Sarah had done and asked her husband for an explanation. No explanation seems to have been given, possibly because Sarah herself interrupted in an attempt to deny her disbelieving reaction to the news. It was of no avail since God is all-wise and does not need to be informed about our behavior.

The birth of Isaac was set for the coming spring, which most likely meant "after nine months."

The fate of Lot's city (18:16—19:29)

As the angelic messengers departed, they looked with anxiety in the direction of the city of Sodom which lay in the fertile plains south of the Dead Sea. Lot had gone there to live when separated from his uncle due to their growing flocks and herds. It was there that the Mesopotamian kings had fought with the kings of the valley and captured Lot. Only by the intervention of Abraham and his allies was Lot rescued and returned to his home in Sodom. Since his nephew lived in the plains to the south, Abraham was deeply interested in what happened there.

The relationship between the Creator and the man He had selected to make the covenant with was growing more beautiful as the years advanced. It was so strong a covenant that the Lord God decided that His intention to investigate the deeds of an evil city should be discussed with His human partner. If Abraham were to be the progenitor of a people who would be destined to bring all nations to their Creator, then he should know something about what was going on. Therefore the Lord told Abraham what He had in mind for the city of Sodom and its neighboring town, Gomorrah. Still in the guise of an angelic-messenger, God pointed out that He was on His way down to the plains to see whether what had been noised abroad about the extreme wickedness of the people were true. If so, judgment had to come.

While the Lord Himself remained to discuss the matter further, two of the angels began their descent into the south country. From the aeons of eternity the angels had been doing the bidding of the Eternal—here they were assigned a special task. They were to look the place over and determine how advanced the evil actually was.

In the conversation which ensued between Abraham and God we see that Jehovah was known well enough to be expected to make a distinction between the righteous and the wicked. This may be the beginning of the concept of heaven and hell, reward and punishment—later to develop into a clear-cut doctrine in the time of Jesus. Abraham argued that "the Judge of all the earth" would do right, that He would not destroy the righteous for what the wicked had done (18:25). To be quite honest about it, he felt rather certain that the city should be spared if only for the sake of 50 good people who lived there. And God agreed. Where there are 50 really committed, God-fearing people, the whole environment can be changed. Jesus did it with 12!

Abraham was a bit uneasy about what he had suggested before, from what was being said about Sodom, it was not likely that 50 good people could be located there. He was somewhat selfishly concerned with Lot and it was clear that there were not 50 righteous persons in Lot's own household. Abraham may have been unsure of Lot himself!

So, with penetrating logic, Abraham pointed out that the figure was arbitrarily set and it would be far from easy to draw a firm line on the number of people it would take to spare the city. Cautiously he mentioned the figure of 40, then 30, . . . 20 . . . and finally 10. In each instance God agreed to be lenient with Sodom. Why Abraham stopped at 10 we don't know. Did he think there would be that many righteous persons in the family of Lot? Or was he afraid to push any further? Whatever the reason, the bargaining ceased and Abraham went back to his tent to await the outcome.

When the two angels who had left Abraham's tent on an errand for the Lord in the land of wickedness reached the gate of Sodom, they found Lot sitting in a position of importance (19:1). "Sitting at the gate" was oriental imagery for holding a place of political leadership. This little insight may inform us that the nephew of

Abraham had done quite well for himself. He had become an elder in the city's government, maybe even the mayor.

In view of the exceeding wickedness of the people, it would have been most unusual for Lot to have climbed to such heights without having made some real compromises. But then, we do not expect as much of him as we do of his uncle in Hebron. Lot was not a part of the covenant, and he may have been out of touch with his uncle Abraham for a long enough period to forget what he stood for. At any rate, he had related to the corrupt city well enough to be elected a leader.

With the same courtesy that had graced Abraham when the angels appeared before his tent, Lot invited the two strangers to spend the night in his home. At first they declined the invitation, choosing rather to remain in the streets. Presumably this was so they could be free to survey the general decadence of the town. When their host insisted that they get off the streets, ostensibly because he knew what they would be subjected to there, the angels went in with him. Lot's wife and servants prepared them a feast. Is it possible that even Lot had begun to sense the real identity of the angelic messengers?

No sooner had they gotten into the dining chamber than the men of the city congregated in the streets outside demanding that Lot introduce them to his guests. We are told that these men were "both old and young, all the people from every quarter" (19:4). Their desire to "know" the guests meant a lust for sexual experience—a terrible perversion. Homosexuality is often referred to by the word *Sodomy* which is derived from the name of this wicked city. God could not abide this deliberate disregard of the divine plan for procreation and oneness of married people. In no way could man cohabiting with man "become one flesh." In the very beginning of creation the Lord had warned man and woman about the responsibility inherent in their sexual powers.

This was not the first misuse of sex, but it was by far the worst.

Any father would find it hard to condone what Lot did. In the effort to protect his guests, he offered his two virgin daughters to the lust-crazed mob to do with as they wished. From what we later learn of the girls, they probably offered no objection. Lot may have been thinking that such an act as intercourse between his daughters and the men of the streets would at least be more nearly normal than what was being asked. And, in the fearful embarrassment of having divine messengers see what was happening, Lot may have just been beside himself in trying to hide the perverted state of his city.

Defying Lot's alternative to their perverted desire, the men rushed upon him in anger. They accused him of being a sojourner, which he was, who was acting like a judge over the natives of the city. Who did he think he was anyway? They had elected him to serve as a city elder, but this was intolerable. If there was anything which they could not tolerate it was a newcomer who set himself up as some kind of saint to tell other people how to live their lives. What they had planned to do to the guests in his house, they now swore to do to Lot as they pressed him against the door with animal desire. At least, this gives rather good evidence that Abraham's nephew had not as yet become a degenerate participant in their sins.

At the very threshhold of violence against his person, Lot was pulled into the house by the angelic messengers and the men outside were struck with confusing blindness, a sign of their spiritual darkness.

Without further delay the divine visitors called for all the members of the household of Lot to be brought together for briefing. Warning was given to their host that the city would be destroyed. Excitedly, Lot sought out his future sons-in-law and told them the news. But they mistook his words for jesting, and laughed. Even Lot himself lingered the next morning as he thought about the flocks and great wealth he would be leaving behind. In mercy, the angels grabbed the hands of Lot, his wife, and his two daughters and forcefully drew them outside the city walls. There, they were told to run as fast as their feet would carry them into the hills. And not to look back! Failure to do as they were told would result in their being consumed.

Fearing that he could not reach the mountains before the heat from the conflagration overtook him, Lot begged to be permitted refuge in Zoar ("littleness"), the smallest of the five cities of the plain. Permission was granted and Zoar was spared. The angels speeded Lot and his family on their way to the city. Not until they were safe there could the angels release their destructive powers upon the city of Sodom.

The sun, which had only been announced by the dawn when the departure from Sodom began, was fully risen when the family arrived in Zoar. Thus, in the morning hours, when it would be visible for miles around, the judgment of God began to appear.

Numerous slime pits (bitumen) surrounded the Dead Sea on either side. The pitch found in them was highly flammable, being a product of petroleum. Sulfur springs were quite prevalent in the area and there was an abundance of salt. It may be that God used an earthquake to ignite the gases which brought about a tremendous explosion throwing salt and sulfur into the heavens to rain red hot particles back on the land.

Archaeology has confirmed that an abrupt catastrophe of some kind destroyed the area south of the Dead Sea 2,000 years before Christ. The Sea has been moving southward during the centuries, and it is usually agreed that Sodom and Gomorrah are now beneath those spreading waters. When Abraham looked toward the plains, he saw the whole district enveloped in black smoke which probably came from the many burning slime pits.

People find it easy to forget. Across the intervening years most of the pagan world had all but forgotten the great Flood. In their smug sinfulness they pursued their idolatrous, carnal ways. What they needed was a reminder that God does not permit continuous, flagrant rebellion without judgment.

Our own world will come to its end in a holocaust of fire (2 Peter 2:6; 3:7,10) similar to that which occurred at Sodom. The ancient conflagration, sudden and irresistible, may have been a "gentle reminder" to the rest of the world. Our Lord warns that the days immediately preceding His return will be like those before the destruction of Lot's city (Luke 17:28-32). Man needs to be reminded again and again of the terrible judgment of God upon sin.

The angels meant what they said: "Do not look behind you . . . lest you be consumed" (19:17, AMP). But the temptation was too much for one of the fleeing party. Lot's wife, unable to turn her back on all that her husband had accumulated across the years in wealth and position, paused at the edge of Zoar to look longingly back upon the exploding town. At that very moment a mass of red hot salt fell from the sky and totally immersed her. It was sudden death. She was literally consumed beneath the molten mass. As the mass cooled, it solidified into "a pillar of salt." Travelers in the sands south of the Dead Sea are shown mounds today which are called "Lot's Wife."

The Disgrace of Lot (19:30-38)

The entombment of Lot's wife in a sarcophagus of salt was not the sole tragedy to follow the wicked influence of Sodom and Gomorrah. Behind the city of Zoar were hills, a whole range of them, where Lot and his two daughters took up residence. What Lot may have been afraid of is debatable. Could it be that the story was soon spread around the city that the fire in the plains had somehow been started by this stranger? It must have crossed the minds of the Zoarites that it was strange for only one family to have gotten out of the surprise explosion. It is also possible that he had bragged about his visitation by the heavenly beings, such bragging only turning the inhabitants of the city against him. Had he come to Zoar to cause trouble, maybe to burn it, too? We do not know the source of his fearful departure from the city, but Lot took his daughters and dwelt in the security of one of the caves.

Centuries before, Noah had disgraced himself by getting drunk and exposing his nakedness to the eyes of his sons. It happened immediately after God had miraculously delivered him from the flood. Now, following the delivery of Lot from the holocaust in Sodom, the use of intoxicants again figures largely in the sexual disgrace of Lot and his daughters (19:32). Aware of the impossibility of finding a husband in a city where their father was suspected, the daughters decided that something would have to be done or they would die childless and their father would have no posterity. Thus, partly to insure the permanence of the family and partly out of sheer obsession with sex, the girls designed a plot to get their father drunk and involved in an incestuous orgy.

Both daughters conceived and bore sons. Moab, son of the older daughter, became father of the Moabites who lived east of the Dead Sea. Ben-ammi, the younger daughter's son, was father of the Ammonites who lived in the distant desert east of the Jordan River. Both nations became, like Ishmael's descendants, bitter foes of the Hebrews.

Continuous trouble with human nature (20:1-18)

How slow we are to learn our lessons. And Abraham was no different. He had gone south to check on the condition of Lot after the disaster which drove the latter into the hills. It was reassuring to know that his nephew had been spared but disappointing to discover the degeneracy of his family. From there Abraham journeyed into the Negeb and spent some time in the area of Kadesh (about 75 miles south of Hebron) and Shur (the vast wilderness to the east). On the way he seems to have stopped for a while at Gerar, a city near the Mediterranean shore about 35 miles southeast of Hebron.

There Abraham made the same mistake with Abimelech, king of Gerar, as he had made many years before in Egypt. He told the natives that Sarah was his sister. Perhaps the same practice of killing husbands in order to confiscate their wives was observed in Gerar. But Sarah was now much older, beyond the age for bearing children, so the taking of a man's sister into a king's harem may have been a method of forming an alliance between kings. Abraham himself was looked upon by this time as a sheikh, maybe even as a king. But regardless of the custom or the reason for the action, Abraham was again guilty of trying to work out his problems without due regard to the covenant and its promises—*and* the Lord of that covenant.

In a dream the king of Gerar was accosted by God who warned him of impending death (in this case meaning sexual impotency) because he had taken a man's wife into his harem. Abimelech reacted quickly to the idea that God would "slay an innocent people" (cut off their reproductive powers) since the king did not know of Sarah's marital state. She had lied to him just as Abraham had. When Abimelech objected to God's punishing the innocent he was using the same logic which Abraham had used with the Lord in their dialogue about Sodom. Pointing out that he had unknowingly taken Sarah but that he had not touched her, the king pleaded for justice. In response, the Lord said that since His own intervention had kept Abimelech from cohabiting with Sarah, Abraham would pray for him to live. But the king was instructed to see that the latest addition to his harem quarters was returned at once to her husband.

Calling Abraham into the royal chambers, the king reprimanded the Hebrew patriarch for having brought the judgment of God upon his people. In reply to a request for an explanation, Abraham gave essentially the same cowardly excuse which we saw in his dealings with Pharaoh. As a compensation for the innocent but near-tragic taking of Sarah from her husband, Abimelech gave luxurious gifts and slaves to Abraham and pledged security for him in any place he desired to dwell within the king's realm. As the patriarch prayed for Abimelech, both he and all his people were healed of their impotency. Life returned to the city of Gerar.

The ways of God are past finding out. From all appearances, we would think that it was Abraham who sinned more than the king. Yet God protected the former and punished the latter. There is no way to explain this except to say that the Creator-Redeemer knows the plan of man's redemption better than we and acts in the interest of long-term objectives. This does not mean that the Lord is unfair, but it does suggest that He has to care for and protect those whom He has elected to carry out the eternal plan. The instruments whom He uses are always so human that the Eternal Spirit must complement their efforts with divine support.

The significant point is that God's perfect plan to create "a people of God" will not be permitted to fail. His kingdom will come and His will shall be done "on earth as it is in heaven." God is sovereign, and in this we can take comfort and hope.

7

EVIDENCE OF THINGS HOPED FOR

Genesis 21:1—23:20

Our God never breaks a promise. Sarah was to have a son in her 90th year. This God had said, and this He would do. The covenant was unconditional, and it would be reaffirmed in Isaac, the son of promise. So when he was born, the aged couple named their new son with a word meaning *laughter*. It was a reminder of their disbelief but also a prophecy of the joy this child would bring them.

On the eighth day, Isaac was circumcised as God had demanded. Even at the age of 90, Sarah nursed the child until the proper time came for weaning him. Indeed, is anything too hard for God?

Wealthy Abraham was accustomed to making feasts. Nothing pleased the Oriental fancy more than an occasion of festivity with plenty of food and drink. On the day of Isaac's weaning (the first stage in his becoming a man), such a celebration was held. But the whole thing was ruined due to the jealousy of Sarah who, seeing Ishmael playing with Isaac, feared the complications which might arise in view of Isaac's chosen place. Abraham was greatly disturbed when she asked that Hagar and her son Ishmael be sent away. There were codes by which decent people lived, and to treat his son by a slave girl with such scorn was neither legal nor right from Abraham's perspective. And we remember how big-hearted he was from the episode with Lot in choosing pasture land for their flocks.

Regardless as to what man's code or his sense of decency may have been, however, God overruled and insisted that Sarah was right—the slave mother and her son were to be sent away. Assurance was given to Abraham that they would both be cared for, and Ishmael, his seed, would father a nation.

With a skin of water on her shoulder and a bag of bread in the arms of Ishmael (the boy would have been about 15 years of age), the two departed into the heat of the desert. The water soon was exhausted so Hagar found a desert bush under which her son could get shelter from the heat. Then, with things looking utterly hopeless, she turned her back toward him lest she be forced to watch him die. But the boy went to pieces at the thought of his mother's heartbreak and began to weep. At once the angel of God (was it Christ?) spoke to Hagar, promising that Ishmael would live and father a nation of people. A spring of water was pointed out to them where they refreshed themselves and moved on.

They lived in the wilderness of Paran where Ishmael grew up, married an Egyptian woman, and brought 12 sons into the world. They would become the fathers of the nomadic tribes occupying northern Arabia. The promise of God was fulfilled.

From the narrative it would be assumed that Abraham soon moved into the land of Beersheba (midway between the Mediterranean and the Dead Sea) which was later to become the southern extreme boundary of Palestine. Every passing year rendered the patriarch from Ur richer and richer. His fields were green and his flocks and herds spread across the land. Abimelech naturally became concerned over his growing strength. As a measure of prevention against being overrun someday by the Hebrew sheikh, the king of Gerar came with his military chief to try to get a covenant between them. He reminded Abraham that he had treated him fairly in the return of Sarah even though Abraham had deceived him. Surely the wealthy patriarch could do nothing less than treat Abimelech and his descendants with the same respect. That day Abraham took an oath which pledged him to honor his pagan neighbors to the west.

There was a matter which had to be cleared up, however, before any such pact could be entered. Water has always been a precious commodity in Israel, especially in the desert sands to the south. The fact that Abimelech's servants had forcefully taken control of one of the Hebrew's wells was a serious affront to Abraham's honor and a threat to peace. Tribes have often been known to go to war over water rights. Reminiscent of his earlier plea of innocence regarding the marital state of Sarah, Abimelech insisted that he knew nothing about the seizure of the well and that he would take care of the problem at once. Abraham then gave sheep and oxen to the king of Gerar to seal the agreement. Seven ewe lambs were set apart as a special witness to remind Abimelech that he had permanently agreed to Abraham's rights to the well he had dug.

It was at that time that the place was named *Beersheba,* meaning either *oath well* or *seven well* (symbolic of the seven ewe lambs). To commemorate the occasion, Abraham planted a tamarisk tree (a sturdy, long-lived species) and called on the Lord God. Perhaps the planting of the tree brought back the fresh thought of the covenant with the Lord—thus he gave God the name *Everlasting.* Or could it have been that the thought of the covenant prompted the planting of the tree as a monument to this milestone in his life? Maybe the covenant with Abimelech initiated the whole idea. No one really knows, but the event which led to an oath to respect one another's rights was a new point of departure for the father of Isaac.

The Supreme Test of Faith (22:1-24)

If Abraham had thought his days since leaving Ur of the Chaldees were hard, he had yet seen nothing of the severity of divine discipline and testing. The most demanding experience of his entire life was impending. It would have been impossible to have believed that the God who was so careful to preserve the life of the son of Hagar would demand the senseless sacrifice of the son of Sarah. Many of the pagans practiced human sacrifice (the Canaanites sacrificed children), but Abraham was certain that the God he served would make no such demands. But there was no questioning the voice and no misunderstanding the identity of the sacrifice which was asked: "Take now your son, your only son, whom you love, Isaac" (22:2, NASB).

The reference to a "burnt offering" may have indicated the totality of the presentation. There would be nothing left.

This was the son for whom the Everlasting God had performed a miracle in the womb of aged Sarah. It was this boy for whom Abaham had prayed, this boy who was to perpetuate the covenant with the Lord forever. It did not make sense at all to hear the Lord demanding the death of a miracle child given to the patriarch and his wife in their old age. Would Jehovah give and then take back? Would He break a promise which had been given and repeated so often? Would "the Judge of all the earth" *not* do right? It was incredible! Nevertheless it was the voice which he had heard before. There was no mistaking that. And it was demanding the death of Isaac.

A good man would have argued with God. But Abraham was not a good man. He was better than that—a godly man.

Without a moment's hesitation (and without a word to Sarah), Abraham called for his son and began to prepare for the climb to Moriah, where the divine voice had directed the sacrifice to be made. Scholars are not definite about the location of Moriah. Tradition has long insisted that the rock of sacrifice was under the temple of Solomon in Jerusalem. That rock is now sheltered by the Dome of the Rock, a Muslim mosque, at the site of the old temple. The Jews believe that the altar of burnt offering in Solomon's temple stood on the exact spot where Abraham laid his intended sacrifice.

From Beersheba to Jerusalem is about 50 miles, a good three days' journey, which is the time lapse noted in the account.

The scene is both tender and gruesome, with young Isaac carrying in his arms the wood to provide fuel for his own death. Gradually it began to dawn on the boy that, while his father had the knife to kill the sacrifice and the torch for lighting the wood, the sacrificial lamb was lacking. In his question, "Where is the lamb?" he was beginning to suspect what must have struck terror in his heart. His fears may have been somewhat allayed when his father said, with great composure and confidence, "God will provide Himself the lamb."

And, indeed, He did.

No words are wasted in recounting what took place at the rough-hewn altar erected by Isaac's father for the burnt offering. We are told nothing about the boy's plea for mercy, nothing about Abraham's intercession on behalf of his son, nothing about the tenderness of those parting moments. Would not the patriarch who implored God to spare the people of Sodom have also done as much for his own son?

With Isaac bound upon the sacrificial pyre, Abraham raised the knife for the fatal plunge of its blade into the quivering body of his son of promise. But the hand of Him who controls the whole world stayed the glistening blade and the divine voice broke the deathly silence: "No! Abraham, no! Your faith has been tested and found reliable before Me! Release your son, your promised heir, and sacrifice the ram behind you." Turning himself about, the shaken father saw, caught in the thicket, a ram which God had *provided* for the burnt offering. At once Abraham sacrificed the ram and gave the holy place a new name: *Jehovah-jireh,* which means "the Lord will provide" (22:14, NASB).

Isaac was a foretype of the Messiah, who would one day be born to his distant offspring. Since the son was probably 16 years old (Josephus says 25), it is unlikely that the agile boy could have been caught and sacrificed against his will. Isaac must have submitted willingly to what had to be done. Thus he becomes a shadow of Him who "became obedient unto death" (Phil. 2:5-8). Abraham himself was a type of the heavenly Father who "spared not His own Son but delivered Him up for us all" (Rom. 8:32). The ram sacrificed instead of Isaac is a faint hint of the substitution of Christ's death for ours, though the analogy is not as clear at this point since God did not find a substitute for His Son as Abraham was allowed to do.

Certainly there is also a foregleam of resurrection faith here in Abraham's assurance given to the servants that he and the lad would "come again" to them. The Hebrews epistle makes note of this faith which was sure that God could bring Isaac back from the dead (Heb. 11:19). It was only a shadow, but at least it was that—a sign of the sacrifice of the Lamb of God which "taketh away the sins of the world" (John 1:29).

Abraham's faith had now been tested to the breaking point without failure. God never intended to see the son of promise slain. The rejection of human sacrifice must have put away the concept from man's mind in the Hebrew nation forever. But it was only when Abraham was willing to give up his only earthly hope of seeing the heavenly promise fulfilled that God was certain that the faith of the patriarch whom He had elected was strong enough, tempered to withstand the rugged tests which would follow. This was the risk taken by the pioneer of faith which proved that the Eternal's choice was not in error. Once again, as the Creator looked upon what He had made, He was able to say, "It is very good!"

At every major milestone in the journey of Abraham, the cove-

nant was confirmed again. We have heard it distinctly three times
in the life of Abraham (Gen. 12:3, 18:18, 22:18) and will come
upon it again in the story of Isaac (Gen. 26:4) and the account of
Jacob (Gen. 28:14). Five times God made the promise to His
founding fathers, a promise which insisted that all nations outside
the covenant would "bless themselves" by what Abraham had believed. This was not only a challenge to the Hebrews to live so that
other peoples would be benefited by their faithfulness, but also a
promise that the surrounding nations would "bless themselves"
on the basis of their attitude toward and treatment of the Jews.
Unquestionably our Lord was referring to the Gentile treatment of
the Jew when He projected the situation at the last judgment:
"Inasmuch as ye have done it to one of the least of these My
brethren [the Jews], ye have done it unto Me" (Matt. 25:40).

The little genealogical account set in the midst of the story of
Isaac and the ensuing death of Sarah seems out of place at first
(22:20-24). We have completely forgotten about Nahor, the
brother of Abraham who chose to stay in Ur when his father left.
Here he comes to light again as having fathered 12 sons (as did
Ishmael later and as Jacob was yet to do), who became the
progenitors of the Arameans who settled widely to the north and
east of the Hebrews. The connecting link between this brief genealogical account and the story of Isaac lies in the passing mention
of Bethuel's daughter, Rebekah, who was a cousin and later wife
of Isaac.

The Family Breaks Apart (23:1-20)
Abraham was 137 years old when death came to his devoted wife
Sarah. Not since the burial of his aged father at Haran had Abraham been confronted with the enigma of death. Losing a wife, the
companion of many years, is far more traumatic than losing a
father. God had said at the outset of creation that man *leaves* his
father and mother and *cleaves* to his wife. In some mystic divine
manner the two "become one flesh" (Gen. 2:24, AMP). Since this
is true, death is a tearing apart of that one marital body. The other
half is forced to exist in an unfulfilling state of non-wholeness.
Because they had lived together for so many years, the separation
which death finally brought to Abraham was unquestionably a new
trial for the aging Hebrew.

Sometime between the episode with King Abimelech in Gerar

and the death of Sarah, Abraham had moved back to Hebron, here called by its older name *Kirjath-arba*. The name had been given to the settlement by the pre-Israelites who lived there before the coming of Abraham. During the time of the Hebrew patriarch a group of these people (called *Hittites* or *the children of Heth*) lived in the area and apparently had their own town government.

Though the entire land of Canaan had been promised to Abraham's descendants, it was imperative that a legal title be acquired for the burial of the Hebrew dead. The living could fight for their rights, but the dead could not. Therefore, a lengthy account of the bargaining between Abraham and the Hittites is preserved for us in this section.

Abraham was actually an outsider, a sojourner in the land. While he was powerful and wealthy he did not own the land itself, and the divine title was not yet respected by the people in political control. In order for an outsider to buy a piece of property under such conditions it was necessary for the city council to agree on the purchase. Having received the permission of the city elders (Abraham was highly respected), the actual bargaining so typical of Oriental commerce began.

A great amount of haggling went on between Abraham and Ephron (owner of the land which was being purchased), much of it under the guise of the usual Oriental generosity. Ephron argued that he did not want to sell his land to so great a man. It would be a privilege for him to give it to him. But Abraham did not want it as a gift which might later be confiscated after his death. He rather wanted a clear title and that could be possible only if the land were legally sold to him.

It is so perfectly clear that Ephron was not sincere in his stated desire to give away his property that the whole story is almost humorous. When the buyer refused to accept it without payment, the owner subtly suggested that a piece of land worth 400 pieces of silver ought not to be a matter of disagreement between friends (23:15). The value placed on the burial site by Ephron was an excessive one, probably 10 or 20 times what the land was worth in that day. Abraham, being in no position to argue, weighed out the amount specified and buried his wife.

What the Hebrew patriarch wanted was the cave opening at Machpelah on the east side of town. This cavernous region would made an ideal place of burial for the family of Abraham. Once the title deed was his, the widowed husband was assured that no one would disturb his dead forever. Even today the traveler is allowed only to look through the opening into the cave but not to enter. Muslims are in control of the sacred burial grounds which they guard carefully.

In the years to come Abraham was to be buried beside his wife. Finally Isaac with his wife Rebekah and Jacob with his wife Leah were also interred with their ancestors.

8
CONTINUATION
OF THE COVENANT

Genesis 24:1—28:9

Isaac Takes a Wife (24:1-67)

In old age one begins to think seriously about his children and what may happen to them. And nothing could have been more important to Abraham than the certainty that Isaac would be properly and happily married to the right woman. (After 4,000 years every father still has the same concern!) No tragedy could be worse than to have the son of promise become enamored with the Canaanite women and marry among the "daughters of men" as the sons of Seth had done. For Isaac to "become one flesh" with an idolator was about the worst thing that Abraham could imagine— and the possibility of such a union had crossed his mind several times after the death of Sarah. He could not face death's approach in peace and quietness unless some assurance could be found concerning a bride for Isaac. For this reason an oath must be taken by someone who could be trusted to represent the family.

Calling for the eldest servant in charge of his affairs (who may have been Eliezer, to whom Abraham earlier thought he would have to leave his possessions), the father of Isaac demanded a serious oath from him. It was an oath which carried a curse in the event of failure to carry it to completion.

The custom of putting one's hand under the other's thigh has been lost in antiquity. It was done to magnify the seriousness of the agreement and may have suggested the curse of impotence if the contract were disregarded.

The servant swore that he would see that a wife for Isaac was selected from among the people in Mesopotamia. It is possible that the household of Terah had abandoned its idolatry upon hearing of Abraham's journey with the God of Shem. The household gods in the tent of Laban (Gen. 31) would tend to disclaim any such hope, however. They just would not have been present among people who were not idolatrous. In the event that no woman would come back from Mesopotamia with the old servant, it was emphatically stated that Isaac must not be taken to Ur or Haran to live. God had given to his family the land of Canaan and Isaac must stay and lay claim to it.

The narrative reads as though the servant left at once on his wife-seeking mission. A caravan of camels was readied, laden with precious gifts for the new bride and enough food for the trip. It was a long journey, and the caravan may have been gone as much as three months. When they arrived at Nahor in Upper Mesopotamia, the shades of night were just beginning to fall. The women of the city would soon be coming to draw water from the well at the edge of town. There the servant waited as he prayed for a sign which would lead him to make the right choice. He asked that the woman whom God had chosen would reply just this way to his request for a drink: "Drink, and I will water your camels also" (24:14, NASB).

God answered prayer that day in such a sudden manner that the old servant was gazing in silence at what he saw, as though he could not believe his eyes. Before the last words of his prayer were gone from his mouth a beautiful girl who was unspoiled by any man came to the well and proceeded to do exactly as he had prayed. The old servant was certain that Rebekah was a very special girl, the one whom God had chosen, due to her willingness to water his camels. (One camel can drink as much as 30 gallons of water. And we do not know how many were in the caravan. To draw water for a number of thirsty camels was no easy chore. Not just any girl would have offered to do that kind of work. Rebekah's action was remarkable indeed!)

Presenting the golden rings and bracelets which he had brought for Isaac's wife, the servant asked for the girl's identity. She was Rebekah, the granddaughter of Nahor himself. Room for the night and food for refreshment were offered by Rebekah—and the servant's mission to find a wife for Isaac was over. After the example of his master, he bowed low and worshiped Almighty God who had granted him such a quick answer to his prayer.

The fact that the girl ran to inform her mother may mean that Bethuel, her father, was dead. Furthermore, since her brother Laban becomes the head negotiator with Abraham's servant, we may presume that this was the case. Later, reference is made to a Bethuel who complies with Laban, but this is probably a younger brother since Laban's name appears first (24:50).

When Laban heard about the stranger and saw the wealth of his retinue, he immediately invited the servant to share his house. Refusing to take food or rest until he had explained his mission, the old servant told the story from the moment he took an oath before Abraham to the instant the girl of any patriarch's dreams appeared. Permission was granted by the brothers for Rebekah to return with the servant to Hebron. Being sad to see her depart, however, the family asked for a 10-day delay. The servant objected and Rebekah was asked to decide for herself. One of the most tender and touching scenes in the Bible is at this point where Rebekah answers without delay, "I will go" (24:58).

In the meantime, either Abraham had returned from Hebron to the Negeb or Isaac had taken leave of his father to travel on his own. Isaac was near Beerlahairoi, the place where Hagar had seen the Lord and still lived, when the caravan approached in the distance with his wife-to-be. When the servant explained what he had done and presented the veiled and beautiful Rebekah to his younger master, Isaac took her to be his wife without questioning either the judgment of Abraham or the wisdom of God. Tersely, but beautifully, we are told that Isaac "loved her" and that she brought comfort to him following the death of his mother.

Thus does God do all things well. Perhaps that very day Isaac explained the covenant which had come to Abraham, how he himself was the son of promise, and anticipated with his new wife the thrilling adventure which awaited them.

Double Trouble for Isaac (25:1—26:33)

Keturah, Abraham's new wife, is called a *concubine,* as was Hagar. She never replaced Sarah, but she did make a good home and give birth to six more sons for the father of Isaac and Ishmael. Her offspring are usually believed to be the ancestors of clans of Arabians to the southeast of the Promised Land. Midian, the most familiar

name, became the father of the Midianites, who later took Joseph
into slavery in Egypt. All the sons produced by concubines were
treated well and given lavish gifts, but they were removed from
Isaac, who was destined to receive the inheritance both materially
and spiritually.

As is often the case in Genesis, the author does not tell the
story in chronological sequence here. Abraham's death is recorded
in advance of the birth of his grandsons who were born when Isaac
was 60 years old. The old grandfather was 100 years of age at the
birth of Isaac and 175 at his death. Therefore he was still alive
when Jacob and Esau were born. But since Abraham does not play
any further role after this point in the narrative, the death and
burial are entered on the sacred page in a running survey of the
genealogy of the generations of his growing family.

Rebekah was barren. Sarah before her was barren, too. The failure to bear children seems to have been attributed to the mothers
in both cases rather than to the fathers. In fact, Abraham had a
son by Hagar before Sarah finally conceived, and six sons by
Keturah after his wife's delivery of Isaac. This clearly reveals that
the problem lay with Sarah. Now we are told that Rebekah had the
identical weakness. Nothing could have been more embarrassing
to an Oriental woman whose prime task was to bear children.

It may be that both these mothers of Israel were barren "that
the works of God should be made manifest" (John 9:3) in them.
Their sons were to belong to Jehovah and were to be conceived by
the direct intervention of Providence. As Isaac prayed for an heir,
Rebekah's barrenness was removed and twins, the first in recorded
history (unless Cain and Abel were twins), were born to her.

Her female intuition told Rebekah that there was something different about what was happening inside her body. A fierce struggle nearly tore her apart, so she sought guidance from the Lord in
fear that she might die. We are not told how God reevaled to her
that she would have twins. But in the revelation was also the prediction that the two sons would continue to struggle against one
another after their births and eventually father two tribes of people
who would become enemies. The strangest part of the divine information was that the older of the two boys would serve the
younger. This was contrary to all custom of the time. But God is
not bound by man's customs or traditions. He knew the qualities
of the twins before they were born and chose the younger to carry

on His plan for a kingdom. God's ways are truly unsearchable. Progress cannot be made without tension. And there can be no tension without something to struggle against. From the beginning the Lord had thrust man into strange but needed situations of struggle. In the garden of Eden there were two opposing trees, representing man's responsible choice. Man was pulled by the Creator on one side and the anti-creator (Satan) on the other. Even Adam and Eve themselves provided an atmosphere of friction for each other. Then came Cain and Abel (later replaced by Seth) with their differences, Noah and his son Ham, Abraham and Lot, Isaac and Ishmael, Jacob and Esau, Joseph and his brothers—struggle was destined all the way. And can we imagine what life would be like without that built-in creative tension which opens the way to growth and progress?

The first son born to Rebekah was called *Esau* (hairy) because he was born with an abundance of hair on his body. He is said to have been *red* at birth, though the description may have had something to do with the *red* pottage which later made him infamous (Gen. 25:30). The word *red* is the root from which comes Esau's surname *Edom;* hence, his descendants were called *Edomites*. They created continuous trouble for the chosen people.

Following Esau in birth was Jacob, whose entrance into the world followed so quickly upon the birth of Esau that he is said to have been grasping the older brother's heel. The name *Jacob* means *heel-catcher* and probably had something to do with the prophecy that he would supplant his elder brother. Some insist that the name more aptly means "he whom God protects." In either case it was prophetic.

Though they were twins, the sons of Isaac had totally different interests. Esau was an outdoorsman who loved to hunt in the wilds. He was a man's kind of fellow and his father seems to have been partial to him. The account explains that the favoritism was shown because Isaac enjoyed eating Esau's game.

On the other hand, Jacob was a quiet man who liked to stay in the tent away from the desert sun and the wild hills nearby. He liked to think and plan, a trait which would serve him well in the days ahead. Because he was at home more, he spent more time with his mother than did Esau, who was hardly ever there. Jacob and his mother grew very close. Rebekah's partiality toward Jacob was as pronounced as was Isaac's toward Esau.

Insight is given into the characters of both boys in the terse account of the bargain made between them on a day when Esau came from hunting in the fields, famished with hunger. What we see makes us dislike both boys. Jacob was deceitful and cunning, ready to take advantage of his brother's need for selfish ends. Thus he made a broth at the edge of the field, the aroma of which set Esau's salivary glands to dancing. When Esau rushed up, complaining that he was "about to die" (an overstatement typical of Oriental hyperbole and still in use today), Jacob offered to *sell* him food in exchange for the birthright which legally belonged to the elder son. Esau was as dull and stupid as Jacob was deceitful and cunning. Who would sell his inheritance for a bowl of stew? Yet that is exactly what he did.

Like multitudes of men and women since his time, he rationalized that man must forget the future and live for *now* since that is all that is certain. What such people forget is that the future holds judgment over the present.

Despising his birthright—that is, considering it unimportant—Esau lightly tossed aside his place in the sun. He had denied himself the honor of bringing forth the Messiah and His kingdom.

Isaac had double trouble with his sons, and we shall look more closely at this later. His "double trouble," however, also had to do with his experience with Abimelech, the Philistine king of Gerar. This may have been the same king mentioned previously in the story of Abraham. Or it may have been his son who had received the royal throne from his deceased father. The latter possibility is more likely.

Isaac had been dwelling at Beerlahairoi in the desert sands. When famine came the Lord instructed Isaac not to go south into Egypt as Abraham had done in such an emergency, but to go north into the city of Gerar (26:2). It was explained to him that the land of Canaan had been promised to Abraham and that Isaac should remain there. The famine was a local problem rather than an areawide emergency as it had been in the early days of Abraham.

At this point the Lord also reaffirmed the covenant which had been made with Isaac's father.

One would think that Abraham, having been in trouble twice due to his misrepresentation of Sarah as his sister, would have warned Isaac not to make the same mistake. Perhaps he did. But the custom of killing men for their beautiful wives was apparently so widespread that everybody with such a wife was overly sensitive. That's putting it mildly! At any rate, Isaac spread the tale that Rebekah was his sister (she *was* his cousin, which relationship could have been loosely termed *sister*) and nearly got himself and the people of Gerar in serious trouble. The deception was discovered when the king happened to see Isaac caressing Rebekah—he knew that this was not the way a man would treat his sister. Abimelech warned the sojourner within his land and shuddered to think what might have happend had one of the Philistines cohabited with Rebekah. No doubt the *guilt* of which the king spoke (26:10) was related to his fear of a curse falling from the God of Isaac upon Gerar. Fearful of Isaac's God, Abimelech pledged to the Hebrew patriarch protection from harm. He would execute any native offender.

Abimelech had not counted on the prosperity which was to come to Isaac, who planted and reaped great and bulging harvests. Soon it was observed that the sojourner was becoming *mightier* than the Philistines (a foregleam of Pharaoh's fear of the Hebrews —Ex. 1:9). The king of Gerar became envious and asked Isaac to depart. It is the ever-recurrent story of the Jews who, not solely due to their wits and business acumen, have grown wealthy and economically powerful wherever they have gone. God has promised and nothing will cancel that covenant. The greatness of Isaac's spirit is shown by his willingness to move on rather than fight when he was admittedly mightier than the Philistine hosts (26:16).

Ancient peoples in desert climates were always having struggles over their water rights. Abraham and Abimelech had found it necessary to enter into an agreement over a well which had been seized from the patriarch's servants by the men of Gerar. Now, much later, the water battle was still under way. Rather than seize the old wells, which may have been too far in the desert to benefit the immediate inhabitants of Gerar, the Philistines filled them full of rocks and sand so the Hebrews could not use them.

With the patience of Job, Isaac set his servants to redigging the ancient wells. But when he found a new spring of water in the valley of Gerar, the herdsmen of the city laid immediate claim to property rights. The same thing took place when he dug into a second stream of water. And rather than become embroiled in war, the magnanimous Isaac gave the wells to the Philistine herdsmen, calling the wells respectively *Esek* (contention) and *Sitnah* (enmity). For some unknown reason the third new well was not contested and the Hebrews called it *Rehoboth* (room).

And for the room to live and grow in peace, the honored son of Abraham gave thanks to the Lord.

Like his father, Isaac was a devout and reverent man. When Isaac arrived at Beersheba, the Lord appeared to him as He had so often to his father, confirming again the promise of the covenant. It was a holy place, so Isaac pitched his tent and dug another well. But, first, we are informed that "he built an altar." While Isaac was there, Abimelech came with his men of war seeking an agreement between the two peoples so there would be peace among them. The king had come once before to Abraham asking the same thing. Maybe the new king remembered his father's act and felt that it would be wise to insure himself by a fresh covenant.

Together they feasted, an Oriental way of sealing an agreement in friendship. As the king and his cohorts departed, the servants came excitedly announcing that they had found water in the well which had been started when they first arrived at the place which Abraham had earlier named Beersheba. Isaac put his own approval upon the choice of names by calling the well *Shibah* (oath). Until this day the name of Beersheba remains.

The Pathos of a Misplaced Allegiance (26:34—28:9)

Esau was "a man of the world" from the beginning. Already he had made it clear that the gratification of his physical appetites was more important than creating kingdoms. Now, 40 years old, as his father had been when he married Rebekah, this elder son chose a wife (26:34). And in doing so he was completely indifferent to the stipulation stated first by Abraham that the sons of promise should not marry pagan women from the land of Canaan. Esau married two wives from among the Hittites who resided at Hebron where his grandmother was buried.

As we would expect, Esau's pagan wives made life bitter for Isaac and Rebekah. Could it be that they jeered and made fun of Isaac's faith and his hope for a great future? Maybe. But the point is more easily discerned in the simple fact that a Hebrew would disgrace his family at the beginning of a long line of anticipated rule. This was enough to make any parents' lives as bitter as gall.

Regardless of what his son had done to bring heartache and disappointment to him, Isaac felt bound by years of tradition to *bless* his elder son. A father's blessing was like a last will and testament in that, once it had been given, it was binding. His eyes growing dim and sensing that death was not far away, Isaac sent for Esau. Is it possible that the ways of his son were primarily responsible for the death of his father? Gray hairs and broken spirits are often the premature results of wayward children who send their parents to early graves.

Isaac requested that his son hunt and kill fresh game, prepare his favorite dish, and return for a meal together. At that time the blessing would be given.

Listening from a distance, Rebekah heard the plans being made and called for Jacob. Carefully she laid out her strategy before him. Deception was in her mind from the first. We may be quite certain that Jacob had inherited his cunning ways from the maternal side of his family! Together the two of them killed and prepared Isaac's "favorite dish" from kids taken from the flocks. Then, with the adeptness of a night criminal, they covered Jacob's hands and neck with the hairy kidskin and dressed him in the "wild smelling clothes" of his hunting brother.

We cannot condone the deceptiveness involved in the treatment of aging Isaac and yet it is transparent from the beginning that God's will was for Jacob to have the blessing. Rebekah and Jacob got ahead of God as Abraham and Sarah had in insuring themselves an heir through Hagar. Jacob suffered all his life for what he did. And so did Rebekah.

Isaac seemed to detect that something was not right when the younger son entered the room. His voice was not that of Esau. Yet the hair on his neck and hands seemed authentic enough and the smell of his clothing had the definite odor of the field upon it. So they ate together and Isaac gave his blessing, which validated the former bargain made between the two sons when Esau sold his right to the father's inheritance.

The blessing assured Jacob of several things: prosperity, national power, headship of the family, and protection from hostile forces. The heart of the covenant concerned the promised kingdom and the reciprocal treatment given to Gentiles who either cursed or blessed the Jews (27:29). It is so until this hour.

At the very moment when Isaac was at last able to lie back upon his mat in peace, knowing that the blessing was now spoken and eternally confirmed, his quietness was shattered with the voice of Esau asking for the blessing. Did this elder brother think that at last he would be able to get "one up" on Jacob for having taken his birthright? If so, it was immediately made clear to him that his younger brother had outsmarted him again. Trembling violently, Isaac declared that the blessing had been given and that nothing could be done about it. Absolutely nothing. With deep anger and hurt in his voice, Esau thought aloud how appropriately his brother had been named—Jacob, the supplanter.

Pleading for a blessing for himself, the defeated elder brother heard the frightening truth that there was little left. Jacob would be the head of the house ruling over his brother; he would father the universal kingdom which would one day produce the Messiah; and he would have at least two-thirds of his father's wealth. But Esau protested in tears. Surely there was *one blessing* for him. So with a heart wrung-out, Isaac repeated Jacob's blessing in reverse upon the elder son: he would not know the prosperity nor the prominence of Jacob; he would live by his sword and serve his galling brother; but the day would come when he would "break loose" from Jacob's yoke.

And so it came to pass. The Edomites, Esau's descendants, revolted successfully against wicked Joram, king of Judah in the ninth century before the birth of Jesus (2 Kings 8:16-22). By the time of Christ, Herod, an Edomite, was king in Jerusalem, reigning over his brother, Israel. However, the Edomites disappeared from the annals of history with the fall of Jerusalem in A.D. 70.

The hatred in the heart of Esau is understandable. But his spontaneous plans to murder his brother put him in the same category as Cain, who was not fit to carry on the family of Adam. As the torch of life was passed to Seth at that early day, so it was passed to Jacob in this later time.

The wisdom of God is past finding out. From before the births of these twins, He knew that Esau would be incapable of the covenant relationship. And we must note that there is a difference between foreknowledge and predestination. The Lord does not compel one to be obedient or disobedient, but He knows what the outcome will be. The distinction may be reserved for scholars in abstruse theology, but the truth remains. God is a sovereign God and no man ever surprises Him.

When Jacob heard from his mother that Esau was making arrangements to kill him, he took Rebekah's advice and fled to Mesopotamia for refuge in the home of Laban, his mother's brother. Rebekah was sure that her eldest son's hostility would cool and Jacob would be allowed to return to the Promised Land. Ah, if only deeds of evil could be forgotten and laid aside so easily! Twenty years were to pass and Rebekah would die before Jacob would return. During those years, Jacob would experience little but trouble.

Before Jacob departed from his father's house, however, Rebekah spoke with Isaac about Jacob's future. She suggested that it would be utter tragedy if he married a Hittite woman as Esau had done. Sympathetic with her feelings, the old patriarch sent Jacob on his way with a blessing—without ever realizing how completely Rebekah had maneuvered his whole life.

As clearly as he knew how, Isaac told Jacob not to marry a Canaanite woman as his brother had done. His mother could not bear up under another episode like that! Instead he must find his wife among his own cousins, the daughters of Laban. This would insure the purity of the bloodline and offset the kind of idolatry which was so prevalent among the people of Canaan.

When Esau discovered what Jacob had done in obedience to his parents, he took a wife from Ishmael's line, a woman who was a paternal cousin, whose mother was an Egyptian. It was a poor and feeble attempt to try to appease the unhappiness which his parents felt toward his Hittite marriages. Even if it could have helped, it was too late.

How pathetic is the story of a misspent life.

9
STRUGGLING
FOR THE COVENANT

Genesis 28:10—36:43

By the time Jacob began his journey to Haran (where Laban appears to have moved; the servant of Abraham had found Rebekah and him at Nahor—Gen. 24:10), Isaac had become reconciled to the choice of Jacob for the next link in the ancestral chain. Rebekah may have talked with her husband for the first time about the prenatal prediction given to her by the Lord. And even though he could not understand it, Isaac knew that what God said would inevitably come to pass.

Jacob's Dream (28:10-22)
Arriving at a place near the town of Luz (about 10 miles north of Jerusalem) as night began to fall, Jacob prepared to sleep. He was all alone, probably because he left in such a hurry, and was unquestionably afraid. The people of the area did not know him, and the darkness only accentuated the sounds and shadows of a strange place. Leaning back against a large boulder, he fought the coming of sleep until his weary eyes would remain open no longer.

Soon came strange dreams. We are surprised that he did not have a nightmare after his treatment of Esau. But God was in the dream and beginning the long process of making a new man out of Jacob.

The imagery of the dream may well have been inspired by the pagan ziggurats (towers) where the idolators worshiped in Mesopotamia. He had probably heard about them from Abraham. They were built in tiers with step-like ledges leading to the abode of the god on the highest peak. The word translated *ladder* means "to pile up" and accurately pictures the firm ledge steps of a pagan tower, not the rung steps of a ladder. "The top of it reached to heaven"—an expression identical with the declared desire of the people who tried to build the tower of Babel.

Angels were all over the towering structure, moving up and down. It was a symbol of the interaction of divine life with human life on earth. Above it all stood the Lord God. That was where one would expect to find deity if he were looking at a ziggurat. This is not to suggest that we have here a *pagan* theophany (manifestation of God by actual experience), but it is to imply that Jacob's concept of God was not personal at this time. The only God he knew was a second-hand deity whose powers and personal communication had been talked about by his father. The setting, therefore, may have been culturally conditioned by the habits of people about him and the stories Abraham had told about the old country *to which he was now going.* The vision, however, was as real a contact with the living God as any experience which had come to Isaac or his father before him. The Lord had revealed Himself in numerous ways, and this was an evidence of His loving power.

From the pinnacle of the tower came the voice of God declaring Himself to be the "God of Abraham . . . and the God of Isaac" (28:13). The terms of the covenant were given to Jacob for the first time—exactly as they had been given so long ago to Abraham. In addition to the original covenant, the Lord promised to be with Jacob while away from Canaan and to bring him back in due time. It must have been awesome to hear Jehovah saying that He would not leave Jacob until He had accomplished what He had set out to do through him. The covenant was unconditional and eternal. The Eternal Spirit would not let one single provision of its terms fail. It is forever.

Awaking from sleep, Jacob was both startled and filled with awesome fear at what had transpired in his sleep. In the twilight zone of his subconscious, he had discovered that God was "in this place" without his knowing it. Has it not been so with all of us? The presence of the Lord is always with us, but it is made more real at special intervals, often when we do not expect it.

Jacob's reference to the place where his revelation came to him as "the house of God . . . the gate of heaven" (28:17) was in keeping with the ziggurat concept which had supposedly made a great impression on his mind. He even named the site *Bethel* (house of God).

Taking the stone on which he had "slept like a rock," he set it aside as a memorial of the event, pouring oil upon it and making a vow to the God who had appeared to him. As Samuel was later to do, he had "raised his Ebenezer" to mark the location where the Lord came down (1 Sam. 7:12). The vow which he made has been construed as an attempt to bargain with God—which would have been characteristic of Jacob! But it is more than likely a sober, humbling admission that he did not deserve any of the great promises listed for him in the covenant. All he felt he could ask was the bare necessities of life: bread, clothing, shelter, and security. This was what a slave was entitled to. And in return for these basic provisions Jacob promised a tenth of all he received in an act of profound worship.

Indeed, to see this spirit in the younger son of Isaac is refreshing. Prior to this time he had spent every waking moment plotting ways to advantageously use other people for his selfish objectives. Miraculous as it may look, a new Jacob was in the process of being born. But the divine transformation was not yet complete.

Jacob Finds an Equal in His Uncle (29:1—31:55)
Jacob meets Rachel (29:1-20)

At the northern extreme in his journey, Jacob approached the city of Haran (about 400 miles northeast of Canaan) where he saw several shepherds with their flocks. They were gathered around the public well which was covered with a stone so large that several shepherds were needed to move it. This was for protection from contamination and to prevent theft of the water. Thus the watering was done en masse when several men were on hand to roll the stone slab aside.

Approaching the place of refreshment, Jacob asked the identity of the shepherds and, learning that they knew Laban, asked about his health. Not only was the Hebrew sojourner delighted to hear of his uncle's health and prosperity, but he was doubly blessed with an announcement that Laban's daughter, Rachel, was coming to draw water. At once he suggested that the sheep be watered and that the shepherds be off with their flocks to pasture. How could a man properly meet a girl who might be destined to be his wife with all that crowd around? But the shepherds explained that none of the sheep could be watered until all the sheep had been gathered. Rachel herself was bringing a flock of her father's and she had not yet arrived.

When Rachel appeared, Jacob excitedly arose and moved the stone from the well. In the wildness of his beating heart, the huge stone became no problem. Like men of every age, he was undoubtedly trying also to impress the young woman with his manly strength. With the stone rolled away, he proceeded to water her father's sheep and, without further introduction, rushed up to Rachel and kissed her. What the shepherds may have thought of all this we are not permitted to know, but at least they must have thought young Jacob a bit impulsive! Of course, she *was* his cousin and the kiss may have been a gesture of kinship. It is doubtful, however, that he would have greeted just any cousin in such a manner.

No sooner had Jacob kissed the lovely daughter of Laban than he broke into tears. His emotions were in bad condition, and his whole being seems to have been shaken at the sight of Rachel. Finally, after the fiery excitement had passed, Jacob got around to introducing himself. Rachel, sharing the thrill of the moment, ran to the house to tell Laban about this "muscular and gentle prince charming" who had come from afar.

A month passed, during which Jacob lived with Laban's family and worked for his uncle, before anything was said about the young man's purpose in being at Haran. When Laban mentioned coming to some agreement about wages for the hardworking son of Isaac, Jacob could refrain no longer from declaring his intentions. He offered to work seven years for the hand of Rachel in marriage, and Laban was predisposed to accept the proposal. His daughter would be getting a good man, and her father would be blessed with a good workhand. We are told that "Jacob loved Rachel" (29:18), and the narrative reads as though it were love at first sight. One of the tender expressions in the Old Testament is that the seven years of hard labor "seemed unto him but a few days for the love he had to her" (29:20).

Laban's deception (29:21-30)

Laban was a businessman, a shrewd and calculating one at that. When the seven years were completed, a great feast was held for the occasion of the marriage of Jacob and Rachel. But during the festivities Laban secretly brought Leah, his *older* daughter, to his nephew and the two of them slept together. The next morning Jacob discovered that he had been deceived, that he had not been with Rachel but with Leah! The account says *her* "eyes were weak" (29:17, NASB), but it would appear that Jacob had the weak eyes rather than his bride! We wonder how he could have spent the night with the wrong woman without knowing it, unless he had imbibed too much wine as had Noah and Lot in their own celebrations. If so, we have another example of the place of intoxicants in a man's troubled life. The girl's veil would not have deceived any but one who was drunk.

Complaining to Laban—and one can almost hear the loud and strident remarks—only resulted in having the custom of the land explained to Jacob seven years too late. The Hebrew prince had failed to read the "small print" in the contract! No father could give his younger daughter in marriage until the older girl was wed. The more credible story is that Laban simply wanted to get his older daughter off his hands before she became a continual "unclaimed blessing" in her father's house.

A second contract was promptly produced by Laban, offering Rachel for *another* seven years of labor! In fact, the "generous uncle" would trust Jacob for the years yet to come by giving him Rachel as soon as the week of wedding ceremonies for Leah was concluded. With little that he could do about the situation (he was alone in a strange land), Jacob agreed.

We sense impending trouble at once when we learn that the son of Isaac "loved Rachel more than Leah."

The birds were coming home to roost. Now Jacob knew how his brother felt when similarly deceived. Now *Jacob* felt how galling it is to be tricked in so important a matter by one's own kinsman. Long before the time of Paul, men were learning that "whatever a man sows, this he will also reap" (Gal. 6:7, NASB).

If anyone is still disturbed by the divine choice of a deceiver like Jacob, he need not be. God cannot choose perfect men to do His work because there are none! But every man must face judgment for the life he has lived, either here or hereafter. For 20 years, Jacob was to know a life of terrible hardship and continual conflict between himself and his uncle. An uncle who was no less cunning than he had been!

The coming of children (29:31—30:24)

Ours is a God of mercy, a fact elaborately confirmed throughout the entire Book of Genesis. Only His eternal love and mercy would have put up with the sins and human foibles of His people. Especially when one was dealt with in a cruel manner, as Hagar and Esau were, the Lord of all the earth did *do right*. And He did not forget Leah, who was unloved by Jacob. The translation which uses the word hated (29:31) is far too strong. A better rendering is *rejected*.

As compensation for her husband's rejection, Leah was made to conceive and bear the first child of Jacob, a son. Rachel, who was loved, remained barren. Here again it should be noted that, like her mother-in-law Rebekah and her grandmother-in-law Sarah, Rachel was unable to bear children until divine providence came to her aid. In each instance, the child who would continue the covenant relationship would be God's specially conceived appointee. In the case of Jacob's sons, they all were chosen. But Rachel's boy was to be used in the most spectacular and significant manner of all.

Leah's first son was named *Reuben* ("look, a son!")—a name which may have been only an exclamation of joy at having a male child. It may also have been sarcasm directed toward Rachel who was barren at the beginning of a contest to see who was the most productive and, therefore, the best wife. The second son was called *Simeon* ("hearing") because God had heard Leah's cry. The third was *Levi* ("attachment") in hopes that Jacob would be drawn closer to his unloved wife. The fourth was named *Judah* ("praised") because the arrival of the child made his mother praise the Lord.

Naturally Rachel was envious. Unable to bear children herself, she asked her husband to "marry" her servant girl, Bilhah, who had been given to her by Laban to bear children for her in the event she was unable. The son born to Bilhah was named *Dan* ("vindication") because God had allowed Rachel to get back at Leah. The second son of the servant girl was called *Naphtali* ("wrestling") since her prayerful struggle against her older sister had won for her.

The contest continued! Leah gave *her* servant girl, Zilpah, to Jacob to produce further children for her since she herself had abruptly ceased conceiving. The son born to this union was given the name *Gad* ("good fortune"). Zilpah's second son was *Asher* ("happy"). It was a running battle all the way.

From the beginning God had not intended that man should cohabit with more than one woman. This was made explicitly clear in the garden of Eden when the Lord brought Eve to Adam. But the fall corrupted *everything,* and man soon degenerated into polygamy, with all kinds of relationships which he rationalized as righteous. Again, it must be observed that God was *progressively* revealing His divine design to fallen man and not demanding a sudden return to the original innocence of the creation prior to the fall. But we see in the jealousy and quarreling which came to the family of Jacob—with his two wives and two concubines—an illustration of why God willed that man should have only one wife.

Leah had outdistanced Rachel in productivity. She and her maid had given Jacob six sons while Rachel's maid had delivered only two. And Rachel none.

To add to the problem, Leah proceeded to have three *more* children. Little Reuben, playing in the fields, gathered some flowers for his mother, Leah, and presented them to her. They were mandrakes (love apples), a narcotic plant believed by the ancients to make one both desirable and fertile. Apparently the sisters alternated nights with their husband—and this was Rachel's night! So in exchange for the mandrakes, the barren wife traded her husband's attentions to Leah for the forthcoming night. When Jacob came in, Leah plainly informed him that he was to sleep with her, even though it was the wrong night of the week, because she had *hired* him. Polygamy inevitably develops the distinct flavor of animalism.

The son born to Leah from this bargain was called *Issachar* ("reward") because she had been well paid for her mandrakes. Soon another, her sixth son, was born and named *Zebulun* ("dowry") since she had now given Jacob enough to make him love her. The almost parenthetical word about her seventh child, *Dinah,* is inserted to prepare us for the further tragedy of polygamy which is related in a later chapter.

In the meantime, "God remembered Rachel" and she finally bore a son named *Joseph* ("may he add") because his birth only whetted his anxious mother's appetite for more children. Though the Lord is credited with her conception (to the Hebrews, God was responsible for everything), Rachel must have henceforth believed even more strongly in the qualities of the love potion in the mandrakes.

By this time Jacob may have had about enough of this wife-to-wife contest which was draining him emotionally in the atmosphere of friction in which he had been caught. Maybe a new location would get the women's minds off their obsession with child-bearing and help the family climate. Furthermore, Jacob was a bit homesick for his father's house and the country where he had been born.

Securing the best of the flock (30:25—31:16)

The request that Laban send Jacob and his family away was customary in Oriental families. The oldest male was, in a very real way, the head of the entire family until his death. Added to this was the fact that Jacob wanted the blessing of Laban so that there would be no hostility in the future due to his leaving. And still another reason for the request lay in the fear that, if Laban were not in accord with his son-in-law's departure, he might forcefully restrain his daughters from accompanying him. It is true that Jacob was wealthy and strong, but he did not want hostilities if he could avoid it. Legally there was no reason why the uncle, who had become his father-in-law, should not permit the departure. Jacob had served his 14 years of labor for Leah and Rachel. The contract had been fulfilled.

It is never easy to turn loose of a good thing. On the basis of every available evidence, God was with Jacob. Wherever Jacob was, there was prosperity. Laban believed that his own accumulation of wealth was because his nephew's mystic blessing remained in Mesopotamia. So he was loathe to let him go. Admitting his need of Jacob's presence, Laban sought to draw up another contract. Jacob could name his wages if he would only stay and work on in Haran. How Jacob could continue to let his mother's brother soak up his blessing and, at the same time, provide the kind of life he wanted for his wives, sons, and daughters was hard to imagine. Perhaps there was a way, however. At once Jacob began to design a method by which he could take advantage of his wives' father.

What he actually suggested sounded to Laban like a better and more advantageous arrangement than his own deceitful plan to get 14 years of work out of Jacob for Rachel and Leah. Realistically, it did not seem that any man in his right mind would give another party to a contract the edge which the younger man was granting the older. But Laban had heard the deal proposed by Jacob with his own ears.

It all had to do with the flocks of sheep and goats. No gifts and no wages were involved. Instead, Jacob would stay and work for his father-in-law for a share of the lambs and kids. He would take all the spotted or speckled sheep and goats and all the black lambs and leave all white sheep and black goats for Laban. Most sheep were white and most goats were black. Thus Laban was getting almost all the flock to begin with, and the nephew was starting with practically nothing. Henceforth, according to Jacob's agreement, any white sheep or black goats found in the flocks would be Laban's. How could anyone reject such a one-sided bargain?

After the deal was closed, Laban treacherously removed the spotted and speckled from the flocks and sent them away under the supervision of his sons. This would make it impossible for Jacob to breed the sheep or goats so as to produce discolored offspring. But he did it!

Modern science dogmatically affirms that what Jacob did to produce discolored sheep and goats is pure myth. It does not work. What the scheming Hebrew did was to cut strips of bark off black tree limbs, leaving them with a striped effect. These were laid beside the watering troughs where the flocks bred. Prenatal marking of the offspring was created by what the flocks saw during breeding time. It was known that the stronger of the flock gave birth in the winter and the weaker in the spring. So the branches with peeled places were used when the stronger bred and were hidden when the weaker did so. Thus the spotted, speckled sheep and goats of Jacob were the stronger ones.

Whether prenatal marking is credible is beside the point. God had promised to make Jacob wealthy and powerful, and He did so. The Lord had given Jacob the sagacity to achieve greatness. Jacob often used it in the wrong way. But remember—Jehovah had made a covenant which He would not break.

Jacob would always be suffering for his selfishness, but the Lord would use Him in spite of it. God uses the best He can find, and it is obvious that Jacob was at least superior to Esau and Laban.

When Laban discovered what his son-in-law had done, he was wide-eyed with disbelief and angry at being outsmarted. Laban's sons were also becoming impatient with their brother-in-law Jacob, and were complaining about what he was doing. News of the deception was all over the village. It was time to go!

Jacob called his wives and explained to them that he had

brought nothing but good fortune to their father and had received nothing from his hand except trickery and dishonor. In addition he assured them that God had been with him, that divine favor proved him to be right, and that the Lord Himself had been responsible for the discolored flocks (31:9). Having been warned to do so by God, Jacob felt it was time to return to the land of Canaan (31:12-13). Rachel and Leah sided with their husband, accusing their father of having sold them (which he actually did) as though they were strangers. Reasoning that whatever "God had taken away" from Laban belonged to them, the two wives encouraged Jacob to do whatever his God directed him to do.

Jacob Returns to His Past Record (31:17—33:20)
The trip home (31:17-54)

Preparations were immediately begun for the long journey into the land of promise. The cattle and flocks were herded out, accompanied by the wives and children on camels. Twenty years earlier (Jacob had served 14 years for Laban's daughters and 6 additional years with the flocks), the supplanter had departed from Canaan—alone. Now he was to return with a large family and tremendous wealth. In the rush of things, Rachel stole the *teraphim* (household gods, which suggest that Laban's household was idolatrous as had been Terah's) and carried them under the saddle of her camel. Even though the people in Mesopotamia were still engaged in idolatrous worship, the patriarchs were destined to get their wives there because they would have been more sympathetic with Abraham's calling than total strangers would.

Some have conjectured that the *teraphim* were stolen because of spite for what Laban had done. Others feel that Rachel needed the security of the deity represented by the little figurines as she moved toward a new world. It may be that she took them as a legal measure since the *teraphim* indicated the legal right of their possessors to the complete family inheritance. Not knowing that the little idols were in the saddle, Jacob fled into the hill country beyond the Euphrates River.

Three days after Jacob's departure, the news was told to Laban, who immediately set out in hot pursuit. Just before he caught up with the traveling caravan a week later (Jacob moved slowly with all the herds and flocks), Laban had a dream in which he was warned not to speak to Jacob at all.

The reason given to Laban for Jacob's fleeing in secret without going through the customary formalities and participating in the usual ceremonies was that the Hebrew was afraid (31:31). In that Jacob was honest, for one of the few such times in his life! But when he was accused of stealing the *teraphim,* an act which had been kept from him by Rachel, Jacob became angry. He assured his father-in-law that the person in his caravan who had done such a thing would die! Searching the tents and belongings turned up nothing. Rachel was apparently sitting on the saddle of the camel, which had been placed upon the ground, and refused to get up because she was in the middle of her menstrual period. By such deception (how insidious was the deceptive influence of both her father and her husband!) she managed to keep the *teraphim* hidden and make Laban look like a fool.

The argument which followed grew more heated as loud and angry accusations were thrown back and forth. Jacob presented before the witnesses on both sides of the family quarrel a running history of the malicious way in which he had been treated and the way God had blessed him in it all. Laban argued that the girls were his, as well as the children born and the possessions earned. It was quite apparent, however, that Jacob had more evidence on his side, so Laban agreed to a covenant which was drawn up on the spot. Gathering stones for a monument, they ate together and heard the terms of the contract.

The pile of stones would be called *Mizpah* ("watchpost"), the spiteful uncle's way of suggesting that God would have to *watch* Jacob lest he break the agreement. Divine surveillance, of course, was needed for both parties, not just one.

The place where the covenant was entered into was called *Jegarsahadutha* by Laban (an Aramaic term for "heap of witness") and *Galeed* by Jacob (the identical term in Hebrew). Each man swore to remain on his side of the watchpost, that Rachel and Leah would be treated well, and that the God of the father of each party and of the grandfather of both would be their judge. Jacob culminated the pact with a sacrifice to the Lord, who had kept His word in the ancient covenant with Abraham and his family.

A wronged brother's forgiveness (31:55—33:20)

The kissing done and the good-byes said, Laban turned his band of servants toward the east where his home was. Jacob proceeded to his father's house in the west. But before he had traveled a day's journey, the angels of Jehovah confronted him. We are not told that they said anything, only that they appeared. Their presence was an assurance that the support of God was to be his as he continued his trip. In honor of the angels who met him Jacob named the place *Mahanaim* ("two armies"). The other army must have been that of Laban's servants. Obviously, the Lord's army had won.

With great fear and anticipation of trouble with a brother whom he had wronged 20 years before, Jacob took every precaution to avoid hostilities. He had left an angry Laban behind in Mesopotamia. Now he was advancing toward an angry Esau in Edom (called also *Seir,* a reference to "hairy," shaggy areas of land) to the south of the Dead Sea. He sent messengers ahead to greet Esau and tell him of his younger brother's great power.

When the messengers returned they brought news that Esau with 400 of his men was moving in the direction of the returning brother's encampment. Not knowing what to make of it, but afraid that it meant war, Jacob divided his people and animals into two groups in order that at least half of his family and flocks would escape Esau's attack. Then he called upon God, thanking Him for the prosperity he had enjoyed (he had left Canaan with only a staff and was now returning with two companies). He reminded the Lord of His promised blessing and asked for divine deliverance from Esau's hand.

Using what diplomatic skill he possessed—and he must have had a great deal of it—he planned to meet his advancing brother with wave upon wave of gifts. Jacob hoped to appease Esau's anger before they had to meet face to face. Here we see the guilt which a man cannot throw off even after 20 years. It still haunted him, and he was still trying to find ways to clear his conscience and save his life. Regardless of all that had happened in the interval, he could not forget his deceitful deed.

Nearly 600 sheep, goats, camels, cows, and horses were sent ahead of Jacob in three different groups with specific instructions to the herdsmen and shepherds. As each succeeding group met Esau the spokesman was to tell the Edomite that the animals were a gift from Jacob, and that Jacob himself would be following soon. By the time Esau reached Jacob, so the younger brother reasoned, he would have been whittled down to size by the display of such prosperity, obvious power, and generosity.

Having sent his servants on to try to buy his brother's friendship, there was nothing for Jacob to do but settle down and get some sleep. The next day would be so demanding that Jacob had to get as much rest as possible. But sleep would not come and he found himself pacing back and forth before the campfire. Finally, he found a place of solitude near the Jabbok, a stream which empties into the Jordan River just north of the Dead Sea. There, he sought the presence of the Lord.

What happened was almost more than Jacob had bargained for. That night was to be remembered as the greatest struggle of his life. At first we are informed that "there wrestled a man with him until the breaking of the day" (32:24). Later it becomes manifest that the *man* was the angel of the Lord, probably the preincarnate Christ Himself. All night they wrestled with one another, for Jacob was a strong and able-bodied man as we discovered in the account which dealt with the single-handed removal of the stone from the well at Haran. When it looked as if he were equal even to this angel-wrestler in power, the divine opponent simply touched Jacob's hip, and the self-sufficiency which had characterized him was over. For the rest of his life he walked with a limp, a reminder of his dependence on the Lord.

Every man has periods of crisis in his life. The night at Jabbok proved to be such a time in the earthly pilgrimage of the son of Isaac. Always before he had been able to work out his problems by human strategy and shrewdness. But at long last he discovered that the strength of man is powerless when used in combat with God, who can disable one by a mere touch. Henceforth he would spend more time in prayer, depending more on the power of divine guidance than on the sufficiency of human wisdom. The narrative reveals that Jacob worshiped with far greater regularity after his night of struggle with the Lord than before. His entire life became more sensitive to God and more concerned with decent interpersonal relationships with his fellows.

Jacob's unwillingness to let the Lord go until He had blessed him is a lucid commentary on his dawning recognition that what a man needs most is the favor of the Lord. Previously he had managed to trade Esau out of the birthright. A little later he connived for his aging father's blessing to validate the exchange of inheritance rights. But now he discovered that none of this was of lasting value unless the *Lord's blessing* could be acquired. Had he waited for that, there would have been no need for his deeds of deception which made him ashamed in the presence of those whom he had wronged. Like his father and grandfather, he too often got ahead of God's leading. He was just so impatient!

To know one's name was synonymous with having some power over the individual. For this reason the Lord would not divulge His name to Jacob. On the other hand, when Jacob revealed his identity the Lord immediately took control of his life, announcing that he would be different from that instant. To mark the difference, his name was changed to *Israel* ("God rules"). This was the name which would be used to distinguish the new people of Canaan from the surrounding pagan kingdoms.

Another milestone had passed in the days of this Hebrew patriarch—undoubtedly the most significant milestone of all. We are not surprised to find that he gives a name to the place where his will was brought into submission to the Almighty. When the angels had met him on his earlier flight from Canaan, he had named the spot *Bethel* ("house of God"). Now, as he returns he names the location of his struggle, *Peniel* ("face of God") because he had seen God's face and lived. It is reminiscent of Hagar's reaction to God's visit at Beerlahairoi (Gen. 16:13-14).

In the distance, Israel (still referred to as Jacob) saw the approaching caravan of 400 men. It was Esau and his servants. At last the moment of reckoning had come. Already we see the change in Jacob. Instead of sending others ahead to reduce the impact of meeting, he went out to confront Esau like a man. He even took special care of the members of his family, putting the concubines with their children in the foremost position, Leah and her children next, and Rachel with Joseph (his most beloved wife and son) in the rear. Supposedly, this was for protection in the order of family importance. It also kept mothers and children together.

Bowing *seven times* (33:3) in the sand was the kind of reverence given to kings. It would appear this humility of Jacob was no longer born out of fear or a false modesty, but that it was a genuine admission of his junior position in the presence of his elder brother.

What had changed Esau's hatred is anyone's guess. Had he simply softened as he matured during the 20 years apart from his cheating brother? Jacob had left in a hurry, it will be recalled, after receiving the patriarchal blessing, because Esau had sworn to kill him. Did the bands of servants and flocks which he met enroute to Jacob's encampment change Esau's mind? Or was it the obeisance given him by Jacob as he bowed seven times, the change of attitude from a cocky rascal to a sobered man, that changed Esau's feeling at the last moment? No one knows. It is a tender scene, whatever the cause may have been, to see a wronged brother, formerly set on revenge, run to embrace one who had cost him everything he had owned of any permanent value. The kissing was only so much Oriental formality, but the weeping of two strong men in each other's arms was a guarantee that both had learned some lessons and that bygones would be left to die of their own accord.

Introductions were made, beginning with the concubines and ending with Joseph. Esau was impressed. When he heard that the herds and flocks which he had met were gifts of appeasement, the older brother refused the offer on the grounds that he had adequate of the world's goods. Jacob insisted, however, and Esau accepted under the pressure of a changed Jacob who, believe it or not, had actually said in honesty, "I have enough"(33:11).

Who would have guessed that he who took advantage of everyone for selfish ends would ever decide that he needed nothing else. Indeed, God had struggled with him and won! What a victory it was. Jacob even called Esau "my lord," an epithet of honor conferred on the older and entitled son in the family. Isaac's elder son could hardly believe his ears, but that was what that "rascally boy" had actually said. The whole scene, as Esau returns home and Jacob proceeds slowly with his caravan, is one of renewed brotherly love.

While Esau returned to the mountains of Edom, Jacob journeyed to Succoth (huts) and "built him an house" (33:17). The name of the place meaning *huts* or *booths,* suggests the kind of quarters erected in the vicinity. Thus, though he was accustomed to living in tents, Jacob may have built a more substantial "lean-to" of tree limbs and skin or brush for his stay in Succoth. Some have suggested that he lived in Succoth several years, but this is unlikely. Succoth was the last stop before crossing the Jordan into the Promised Land, about three miles east of the river. Nearly 20 miles farther on, on the west of the Jordan, Jacob bought a piece of property in a city of Shechem. He called the property, which he acquired for "an hundred pieces of money," *El-Elohe-Israel* (God, the God of Israel). This may connote a dedication of the first parcel of ground to be legally owned by Jacob in the Promised Land to the God who had brought the sojourner back, as He had been asked to do much earlier at Bethel.

Disgrace in the Family of Israel (34:1-31)

Thus far we have seen a faint hint of homosexuality among the ancestors of the nation of Israel (Canaan in Gen. 9:22-27), a clear-cut case of incest (Lot, Gen. 19:30-38—though Lot was not in the direct line of descent), and repetitious polygamy (Gen. 16:34; 25:1; 28:8-9; 29:21-30). Now we come to our first record of rape (which may or may not have been fornication, depending on the attitude of Dinah). In every instance the sinful attitudes not intended by the Creator were the outgrowth of man's fallen nature. We don't like the events, but we thank God for an honest report.

Mention has been made of Dinah (Gen. 30:21) in order to prepare us for this incident. She was the daughter of Jacob by Leah and her name means *judgment* or *judged*. The account plainly states that she was seized by Shechem, son of the leading citizen of the city, and forcefully raped (34:2, NASB). Her name would suggest, however, that she may have had some guilt and was thus judged by what happened. Of course, the judgment spoken of may refer to some act of divine displeasure brought about in Dinah's life due to the waywardness of the family. This is assuredly pure conjecture and has no evidence to support it either way.

After Shechem (a Hivite member of the Canaanites in the land before the coming of Joshua) disgraced Dinah, he apparently fell in love with her and began preparation through his father, Hamor, to have the two fathers discuss marriage. But Jacob and his sons heard of Dinah's defilement before Hamor called upon them. As a result, they were in no mood to talk of marriage.

Hamor may have caught Jacob's sons a bit by surprise when he asked not only for the hand of Dinah in marriage to his son, but suggested that the whole clan of Israelites intermarry with the Hivites. This would insure the Israelites a place in the land where they were still sojourners and, though not stated for obvious reasons, would insure the Hivites a share in the Hebrew's fabulous wealth. Shechem offered the usual generous gift if allowed to marry Dinah.

The narrative explains how the sons of Jacob set about to

deceive the Hivites just as their father had deceived practically everybody he met. The proneness to deceit was deeply rooted in Jacob's sons! Simeon and Levi, the sons later named in the massacre and probably those who plotted the cunning move, were the sons of Leah, who was substituted for Rachel at the marriage of Jacob. This would suggest that Leah was a knowing party to Laban's evil deed and thus as deceitful as both her father and stolen husband. If so, the sons inherited their tendencies for this kind of thing from both parents.

What Jacob's sons did was agree to the marriage of the two peoples on the condition that the Hivites be circumcised as were the Israelites. A town meeting was called at "the gate of the city," explaining the affluence which would come to the Hivites for so little and short-lived an inconvenience (34:23). The idea sounded as fool-proof to them as Jacob's bargain about the striped and speckled sheep had seemed to Laban. So they agreed to the terms, and every male was circumcised.

Two observations need to be made. One is that the brothers plainly stated that unless the terms were agreed to they would take Dinah and leave. There would be no legal action. This was because it could not be proved that Dinah was innocent and because she had gone out alone, a fact which made her open prey for any man.

The other observation is that Jacob seems to have known nothing about what the two sons were planning. Later he rebuked them (Gen. 34:30-31) and at his death he referred to what they had done in bitterness (49:5-7). This would lucidly point out the change in the character of Jacob since his struggle with God at Peniel. Prior to that time, he would have been totally immersed in the original plot and inordinately proud of sons who were so capably shrewd.

Three days after the mass circumcision of the Hivites, two of Dinah's brothers, Simeon and Levi, sneaked into the city and killed every male with the edge of the sword. Normally two men could never have accomplished such a task, but the pagan men were in no condition to move, much less fight. Dinah, who had presumably been held captive in Shechem's house (either with or without her consent), was rescued and returned to her people.

Hearing what had been done, the other brothers came to plunder the city and carry away the Hivite women as slaves. When Jacob complained that such a deed would bring down the wrath of other

Canaanite inhabitants upon the Israelites, Simeon and Levi could only insist with vehement anger that their sister was not a harlot. Such treatment could not be tolerated.

Sorrow as an Aftermath to Disgrace (35:1—36:43)

From Shechem the Hebrew caravan moved south to Bethel, where Jacob had his dream of the tower steps and saw the angels of God going back and forth between the heavens and the earth. The southward trip was made under specific divine instructions. The patriarch was even under direct orders to build an altar upon his arrival there (35:1). Aware that this was to be an important step in the life of the embryonic nation of Israel, Jacob explicitly demanded that all "foreign gods" be put away. These included the *teraphim* which Rachel had taken from Laban, but there may have been others as well. The golden rings from their ears were given to Jacob along with the idols. He buried them beneath the *terebinth* (oak or evergreen) at Shechem, possibly the same tree Abraham had visited much earlier (Gen. 12:6). The burial probably signified the death of the old gods and all trinkets associated with their worship.

All the people were then instructed to change their clothing and wash their bodies as an act of sanctification or ceremonial purification by which they would be ready to appear with Jacob at the holy place in Bethel.

Everywhere the family of Israel went, the protection of God was with them, even as had been promised at Bethel 20 years before. The protection came in a kind of reverse fashion in that the servants of Jacob did not need to lift a finger to defend themselves. The pagans were terrified of their presence and dared not molest them. At Bethel, Jacob built an altar as God had instructed, calling it *El-Bethel* ("the God of Bethel"). It was another act of dedicating a parcel of ground to the Lord, who had promised Abraham that the total land of Canaan would someday belong to the chosen people of God.

While at Bethel, the aged nurse of Rebekah, Deborah, died and was buried beneath an oak which Jacob named *Allon-bacuth* (oak of weeping). We do not know how Deborah happened to be with the family of Jacob, but we do know that she must have been dearly loved, though a slave.

At Bethel, the Lord appeared again to reaffirm the covenant.

Once more, as at Peniel, the significance of the change in name from Jacob to Israel was emphasized. The Peniel-Bethel change of Jacob to Israel was symbolic of a new future. Just as Abraham and Sarah experienced name changes at a new place of beginning in their lives. The covenant was a confirmation of the promise which had been given first to Abraham and then to Isaac, the father of Jacob. We are told that Jacob (Israel) set up a stone pillar over which he poured oil and wine as a *drink offering*. This may have been the same pillar which he had set up almost a quarter of a century earlier when departing from Canaan in fear of Esau. If so, travelers and vandals may have desecrated the former monument, scattering the stones over the ground. Its significance would have been meaningless to everyone except Jacob.

At a distance from Ephrath (short form of Ephrathah, original name of Bethlehem), it was reported that Rachel was in "hard labor" (35:16). Jacob's twelfth son was born, possibly beside the road in a makeshift "lean-to" as protection from the weather. In giving life to another, the girl for whom Jacob had worked 14 years died. In Rachel's last breath she named her new son *Benoni* ("son of my sorrow"). Apparently the boy's father was not happy with such a sad name so he changed it to *Benjamin* ("son of the right hand"). He may have felt that this, his youngest son, would be his best support and, as Jacob had done himself, would supplant the older brothers. This latter speculation is not deserving of much credence, however, in view of the favoritism which was to be shown to Joseph.

Rachel was buried beside the road and a tomb constructed to mark the site.

Journeying on toward Hebron, his heart broken over the death of his beloved wife, Jacob pitched his tent near a tower called *Eber*, midway between Bethlehem and Hebron. It was during the stay at Eber that Jacob's heart was to be broken by the report of his son Reuben's adultery with Bilhah, the concubine given to Jacob by Rachel. Reuben was his oldest son, the first-born of Leah. He was denied the birthright because of his evil deed (1 Chron. 5:1).

Following this unhappy episode in the life of Jacob's family is a genealogy of his sons with a brief reference to his arrival in Hebron, the death of Isaac at 180 years of age, and the interment of their old father by both Esau and Jacob.

Chapter 36 steps aside from the narrative of the covenant line, to give a genealogical account of Esau, who will henceforth figure little in the history of Israel except as tribal antagonist. The differences in the names of Esau's wives can best be explained by assigning more than one name to the same woman, not an unusual custom. A brief interlude is included regarding "Seir the Horite" whose people inhabited the land to the south of the Dead Sea before Esau came to rule.

When it was determined that Jacob and Esau could not dwell together because of their increased flocks (reminiscent of Abraham and Lot at Sodom), Esau moved permanently to Edom or the Mount of Seir. Thus Jacob was recognized as the rightful heir to Canaan. The listing of *kings* in Edom prior to the kingdom of Israel was that of tribal ancestors while the *chiefs* probably ruled over specified areas of land.

10
DREAMING
OF A KINGDOM

Genesis 37:1—41:57

The Stage Is Set (37:1-11)

At the tender age of 17, Joseph was helping his older brothers Dan, Naphtali, Gad, and Asher tend the flocks. These were all sons of concubinage—nothing is said of Leah's boys, or of Benjamin who was only a child. We are not told what the evil report was which Joseph gave his father about his half-brothers (Gen. 37:2). It's possible that Joseph was spoiled and glad to get attention by getting his brothers in trouble. But it's more probable that they had been involved in some kind of mischief which the younger boy believed should be reported. Our first hint of his being disliked by his brothers is at this time when he squealed on them. It was quite normal for them to react as they did.

In addition to his being a tale-bearer, Joseph was favored by his father above the rest of the family. There was no doubt about it since Jacob had made it plain and unmistakable by presenting to "the son of his old age" a special robe. Some translators have rendered the descriptive words about the garment as referring to *long sleeves,* others as having reference to a kaleidoscope of *colors.* The important thing is that the coat was a symbol of prestige, a distinction which none of the brothers could overlook. Every time Joseph appeared—and he invariably wore his "irritating" robe—it was as though he were gloating over his preferred place in the father's affections. And they hated him for it! In short, there was no chance of brotherhood or peace under such conditions.

Of note is the reference to Joseph as "the son of his old age" (37:3) when, in reality, he was not much younger than the other 10 and was older than Benjamin. The statement must be read in light of the fact that Joseph was the long-awaited son. He was the firstborn of Rachel, Jacob's chosen, special wife, and was not born until all the other wives had borne their sons. For a while it looked like Rachel would never have a child. Therefore when she did conceive, it was to be expected that the child would be considered something special. Actually, Jacob was an old man when *all* his sons were born.

Joseph should have known that his brothers were envious of him and intolerant of his attitude. But he only made matters worse by telling them about his egotistic dreams. The first dream was of the 11 brothers' sheaves (which they were cutting in the field) bowing to Joseph's sheaf. Its obvious symbolism denoted his superiority over his brethren. It sounded to them like a nightmare rather than a dream!

The second dream was of the sun (Jacob), moon (whoever was serving as his mother), and the 11 stars (a zodiacal reference to his brothers) bowing to him (obviously the twelfth star in the zodiac).*

Even Joseph's father was disturbed by the second dream and rebuked him mildly for such an attitude. Yet, while the brothers became even more jealous, Jacob "kept the saying in mind" (37:11, NASB). It was as though he knew this son was destined for greatness, like Mary who, concerning Jesus, "kept all these things and pondered them in her heart" (Luke 2:19). The dreams, galling as they must have been to the rest of the family, may have been God's way of preparing them for what was soon to happen.

A Kingdom Sins Against Itself (37:12-36)
Having heard that pastures were greener farther north, the sons of Jacob drove their flocks into the country of Shechem, where disgrace had come sometime earlier to Dinah. It was at Shechem that Simeon and Levi had massacred the entire male population. Many

---

* This is not to say that Joseph was ever a participant in some astral cult. Such divining of the future by the stars is forbidden in Scripture (Isa. 47:12-14; Jer. 10:2; Zeph. 1:4-5). No evidence exists for assuming Joseph was even remotely engaged in astrology. He was aware, however, of the cultic practice by peoples of his day and relates his dream in the imagery of that pagan idea. This no more suggests his involvement with the astral cult than Jacob's dream of a ziggurat (Gen. 28:12) suggests an affinity by him for ancient observatory star-worship at those pagan towers.

nights, under the starlit skies where they watched the sheep and goats, they must have relived their wild and brutal deed wtih fraternal pride and mirth.

Concerned for the sons' well-being, Jacob called young Joseph and sent him to Shechem to inquire about their needs and return with a report. Arriving at Shechem to ask the townspeople, he discovered that the shepherds and their flocks had moved still farther north (about 15 miles northwest) to the town of Dothan. The name means "two wells" and the place was probably good for watering flocks. It is known that the area was superb for pasture. There Joseph found his brothers and the epic story of his life as an alien began.

Seeing Joseph approaching, one of the older brothers insisted that the time had come for killing the hated "dreamer" and putting an end to his conceited tales. Reuben, the firstborn of Jacob and rightfully in charge at the time, objected to any such unfeeling cruelty. Making it appear that he was not totally opposed to doing something with the boy, Reuben agreed to imprison him in a dry pit from which he hoped to later free him. So the brothers confiscated his treasured "coat of colors" and threw him into the pit. The angry brothers taunted Joseph, made fun of his coat, threatened him with death, and refused to share their coarse food with him.

Judah, Jacob's fourth son by Leah, was the first to come up with an idea of how to dispose of the young dreamer without murdering him. Seeing an approaching band of Ishmaelites from Gilead bearing their products to be traded in the markets of Egypt, Judah hit upon the plan of selling the boy to them as a slave. (The Ishmaelites were descendants of Abraham's son by Hagar, the concubine. They were the ancestors of the Arabic nations.)

Acting as though he felt a twinge of humaneness toward his "own flesh," Judah actually was thinking of the profit they could make on such a deal. It was the same kind of momentary materialism which had caused Esau to sell his future with the explanation, "What profit is my birthright to me now?" So Joseph was sold for "20 shekels of silver," the price of a slave (37:28).

Of particular interest is the fact that it was Judah who made this proposal to dispose of Joseph. He had more reason for wanting this "dreamer" out of the way than the others. Reuben was disqualified from the birthright because of his adulterous incest, and

Simeon and Levi were rejected because of their murder of the men of Shechem. Judah, the fourth son, was next in line for the family birthright. Joseph was the favorite son of his father, however, and the firstborn of Jacob's favorite wife. The "coat of colors" and the strange dreams only served to convince Judah that he would be displaced by the younger boy. Selling Joseph into slavery was the best way he could imagine for making sure that the birthright would be his.

Much later the descendants of Judah and Joseph were often rivals for the place of power in Israel. Judah was supreme in the days of David and Solomon. Later 10 tribes seceded under the leadership of Ephraim, a son of Joseph.

When Reuben returned from checking the flocks, he found that the boy was gone. In bitterness and remorse he explained that he was responsible for the family and for him to have allowed such a thing to happen would bring down the wrath of Jacob. But the sly sons of Jacob were not to be outdone. Dipping the "coat of colors" into a goat's blood, they took it to Jacob for his own appraisal of what had happened.

It was obvious to the old father that his Joseph had been slain by a wild beast. In sackcloth and grief he fell upon his face in mourning. He refused to be comforted by his sons and daughters. In his despair Jacob anticipated the time when he would go "down to Sheol" in sorrow. This is the first mention of Sheol, the place of departed spirits, which was to develop into a concept of much importance.

The reference to Midianites having sold Joseph to Potiphar in Egypt would suggest that the Ishmaelites and Midianites had already intermarried and were thus known by either name.

Judah Goes from Bad to Worse (38:1-30)

Sometime after Joseph had been taken to Egypt and the days of his mourning were past, Judah visited a certain Hirah who lived at Adullam, a village settlement southwest of Jerusalem in the foothills. The Adullamites were one of the tribal units of Canaanites living in the land promised to Abraham. One may presume that Hirah was a friend of Judah and that the occasion of the visit was a business concern. While there, Judah was enamored by a Canaanite woman, daughter of a man named Shua, whom he married. No word is offered about how Jacob may have felt about this, but we can be certain that he did not approve.

Three sons were born to Judah: Er, Onan, and Shelah. Though Judah was not concerned about his father's wishes in the choice of his wife, the headstrong son was determined that his own boy would be properly married. So Judah selected a woman named Tamar to be the wife of Er. Due to the wickedness of Er (we do not know what it was), the Lord did not allow him to live.

The concept of levirate (brother) marriage (Deut. 25:5-10) was clearly already in operation in the days of the patriarchs. This custom was designed so that a man would not remain without descendants in the event of his death before the birth of children. His wife, under such circumstances, automatically became the wife of the next younger brother, who was expected to produce a son for the deceased husband. Therefore, Onan was told to do the duty of a brother-in-law. Knowing that the offspring would not belong to him, but to Er, Onan refused to culminate his sexual act in a proper way and is said to have been put to death by the Lord. How this may have happened is not recorded.

Fearing that Tamar was somehow a cause of the deaths of his sons, Judah asked that she remain a widow until Shelah was old enough to marry her.

Following the death of Judah's wife, he and Hirah joined the shepherds in the village of Timnah to shear sheep. Tamar, hearing that Judah was departing for the fields, laid aside her widow's clothing and draped herself with the veil of a prostitute plying her trade. Seating herself at a place of entrance where she knew her father-in-law would pass, she waited for her chance.

Tamar took this course for several reasons. First, she was angry because Shelah, who was now matured, had not come to her as agreed upon in keeping with the levirate custom. Second, she was growing old without children for either herself or Er. Third, to seduce Judah would both give her the desired offspring and pay him back for his mistreatment of a waiting widow. Fourth, the period following Judah's wife's death was a vulnerable one for him both physically and emotionally, and Tamar knew how to take advantage of it.

When Judah saw her and mistook her for a prostitute, he sought to make arrangements to avail himself of her services. Since he had no goat with him—the agreed payment—Tamar demanded a pledge of payment. The pledge, upon her suggestion, was his staff (an item which changed hands in business transactions) and his seal and cord (the seal being a personalized means of identification worn on a cord). There was little monetary value in these objects, but they were chosen in order that she might later prove the identity of her child's father. Following the shameful act, Tamar reclothed herself in her garments of widowhood and returned home as if nothing had happened.

Hirah, the Canaanite friend of Judah, was to serve as go-between in delivering the goat to the prostitute. When he inquired after the harlot (a "profession" apparently not frowned on by the local citizenry), no one had seen such a person (38:21). Upon hearing of the embarrassing situation, Judah decided to drop the whole matter lest it create further confusion and ridicule. After all, he had tried to pay his debt and the loss of the pledge, though unfortunate, would have to be accepted.

Three months later, Judah heard that Tamar was pregnant. He was sure that she had become promiscuous and ordered that she be burned for her sin. But when she held up his staff, seal, and cord in the presence of the people, claiming that they belonged to the undelivered child's father, it was plain to see that Judah was caught. Admitting that she was entitled to Shelah and that the rightful husband had been withheld, Judah confessed that he himself was the worse of the two sinners. Though he had been tricked, he had nevertheless descended into an immoral act as well as dishonored both Shelah and Tamar.

When Tamar was delivered she gave birth to twins, named *Perez* ("breach") and *Zerah* ("dawning"). Though the hand of Zerah is said to have appeared first (a scarlet thread was attached to it for identification of the firstborn), Perez bypassed his brother and became the rightful heir. Thus he was called *breach*. In a sense we have here a similar situation to the prenatal struggle of Jacob and Esau. Perez, too, became a supplanter.

The story of Judah's shame is entered here for two reasons. First, it shows how sin, once it has begun its course (the selling of Joseph and even prior to that the murder of the men of Shechem), carries one from bad to worse. Second, it reveals how God, being forced to use man in his fallen state, is able to overrule in His own good time. Perez is listed as an ancestor of the Messiah Himself (Matt. 1:3, NASB). While we cannot condone Judah's or Tamar's sins, we must stand amazed at the sovereignty of God and the

unconditional nature of a covenant which He would not allow to
be annulled. Heis, indeed, a God of wonder.

The Dreamer Becomes a Governor (39:1—41:57)
Head slave at Potiphar's (39:1-23)
As the Lord designed, the caravan of Ishmaelites sold Joseph to
a high ranking officer serving as captain of Pharaoh's guard. His
name was *Potiphar* ("whom the sun-god has given"). Joseph was
a good and obedient servant in the household of his master, one
who served well wherever he was placed. Like his father before
him, everything he touched seemed to prosper. So Potiphar took
note of that! We are informed of Joseph that the Lord was with
him and that this is why he was successful (39:2). Even the
Egyptian military officer sensed that the divine hand was upon him.
This master was so pleased with Joseph's capability in managing
the affairs of the house that he put him in complete charge of
everything. This may mean that he was overseer of other slaves as
well as tangible property.

Abraham, Isaac, and Jacob had been tested to determine their
worthiness. Now it was Joseph's turn. Thus far he had lived a
rather protected life as the favorite son. Though being sold into
slavery must have been an emotional trauma for him, he quickly
recovered and found life rather satisfactory in Potiphar's house.

Now the time had come for Joseph to be exposed to the severi-
ties of the pagan world, to be put through the grind of temptation.
Note is made of his handsome appearance (39:6), which was more
than Potiphar's wife could resist. Without shame or hesitation she
brazenly asked the head slave to lie with her. Out of respect for
his master, who trusted him, Joseph refused her daily insistence
that he respond to her desire. The main reason for his firm resistance, however, was because he did not choose to "sin against
God" (39:9). At this early moment in his life, we become aware
that we are face to face with one of the rarest and choicest speci-
mens of devout manhood in the Old Testament.

Not to be rebuffed and humiliated (as the wife of so great a man
she was probably pampered and spoiled), on a day when the other
servants were out, she grasped Joseph's clothing and insisted he lie
with her. Out of godly fear the young man fled from the quarters,
leaving his garment in the hands of the determined woman. She
was so angry at her failure and embarrassed by Joseph's purity that

she cried out to the servants outside, claiming to have been attacked by the Hebrew slave. When Potiphar returned home she told the same lies to him, lies which led the master to throw his servant into prison.

The fact that Joseph was not killed may imply that Potiphar suspected his wife's inclinations. His behavior was so exemplary in prison that he was given authority over the other prisoners. And his relationships with the prisoners and the warden were of such nature as to command respect from all.

A prisoner with divine powers (40:1—41:36)

Kings are easily offended. Pharaoh was displeased with two of his most highly-placed servants. The chief baker and chief butler were both in positions of trust which demanded the greatest possible loyalty to the king. How easy to poison a king or sabotage his rule from inside the royal palace! What these two servants had done was deemed worthy of incarceration, so Pharaoh had them placed in the prison where Joseph was a trusted inmate. When the butler and baker were committed to Joseph, the Hebrew youth was in a position to be noticed by the king himself.

One morning the two officers (though they were servants, they were "chiefs" in their respective tasks) were downcast because they had dreamed during the night and, being in prison, had no access to wise men of the court who could interpret the strange mental pictures. Portents, dreams, visions, and all inexplicable phenomena were very important to people in ancient times. The mere mention of dreams set Joseph's mind to work, for he had enjoyed a few significant dreams himself! Believing that dreams were given by God and, therefore, interpreted by Him, the prison trusty suggested that the king's officers might find help if they would describe what they had experienced in their sleep.

The butler told his dream first. A vine with three branches, on which blossoms and full-ripe grapes appeared suddenly, had appeared to him. Immediately the butler had pressed the juice from the grapes into the king's cup and put it in the hand of Pharaoh. At once the whole thing was clear to Joseph. In three days the butler would be restored to his position and his head would be held high. He would be cleared.

The baker's dream revealed three bread baskets on his head. The birds were eating food which belonged to the king out of the baskets. Again, without delay, the vision was clear to young Joseph. In three days the baker's head would be lifted high too—on the limb of a tree! The king would have him hanged and the birds would eat his flesh.

Sure enough, three days later, at a birthday celebration for Pharaoh, Joseph's interpretations came true.

Joseph had asked the butler to remember him to the king in order that he, too, might be exonerated and released from the prison. Too often, in the joys of freedom and prosperity, we forget those who have helped us arrive at our place of power. True to this form, the chief butler forgot all about Joseph.

Two long years later, the king himself dreamed, and all the court was in an uproar. Someone had to be found quickly who could relieve Pharaoh's mind about what to expect regarding his dream. Standing by the Nile River, the source of the canals which brought productivity to the sands of Egypt, Pharaoh saw seven fat cows emerge from the waters. They were instantly followed by seven lean cows, which devoured the fat ones. A second dream was very similar and emphasized the importance of the experience. Seven full ears of corn on one stalk were eaten by seven blighted ears on another which had been devastated by the fierce, east wind. Describing his dream to the royal magicians and wise men, Pharaoh became incensed against them because they could not make sense of it.

Suddenly, after two years, the butler remembered how Joseph interpreted his own dream in prison. Joseph had long been faithful over a little; now he would be set over much (see Matt. 25: 21).

Called from his imprisonment, Joseph groomed himself to appear before the king, who demanded that his dreams be explained. With gratitude to God, the young Hebrew made a point of the fact that he had no powers of his own, but that God alone could solve mysteries beyond the reach of human intellect. The two dreams were related in detail and Joseph discerned that both of them were saying essentially the same thing: seven years of plenty would be followed by seven years of famine. The fact that the dream was repeated twice, with only a variation in the symbolism, was evidence that God had fixed the matter and no one would be able to alter the course of the years.

Joseph advised that 20% of all which would be produced during the first seven years should be stored so that food would be available during the famine. Furthermore, he suggested that a man of discretion and wisdom be set over the program of food production and storage.

From rags to riches (41:37-57)
The whole idea sounded like an answer from the "gods." Pharaoh liked it, so without delay it was put into effect. Joseph himself was declared the wisest man in the kingdom, a man filled with a divine spirit. Thus it was only natural that he should become the one to govern all plans and the implementation of them. A chain of gold was draped around his neck—it was a decoration given to those who had been especially helpful to the pharaoh. The signet ring from the royal finger was placed on Joseph's hand, indicating the power of his office. The second largest carriage in the land was at his disposal. Everywhere men bowed before him.

Since Joseph was apparently possessed by a divine spirit, he deserved a religiously oriented wife. Asenath, daughter of the priest at Heliopolis (On), was given to him, and his name was changed to *Zaphnath-paaneah,* an Egyptian tongue-twister which had to do with Joseph's ability to sustain the land and its life during the famine.

God blessed all that Joseph did, and the harvests were so abundant that the Egyptians lost track of the massive quantities stored in the granaries. But the Lord blessed him in other ways also. Two sons were born to him: *Manasseh* ("making to forget") and *Ephraim* ("fruitful"). At last the misery created by his brothers at Dothan was forgotten, and his life was beginning to count in preserving the nation and providing descendants for himself. When the famine finally began, Joseph opened his storehouses and rationed the food to Egyptians and foreigners alike until the famine was past.

Joseph was only 30 years old when he was promoted to second place in the kingdom. He had spent 13 years in servitude. The rapidity with which he was elevated from prison to power, from rags to riches, must have made his head swim. He had proved himself faithful and God had honored him.

But the grandest act of all was yet to be. In the succeeding section we shall look at the magnanimity of this son of Jacob.

11

A NATION BORN IN FORGIVENESS

Genesis 42:1—46:34

Two Trips to Egypt (42:1—43:15)

In times of famine in the east, large areas were usually involved. The devastating effects were far-reaching, and most of the nations surrounding "the land of the Nile" soon felt the pangs of hunger.

Jacob's sons in Canaan were rebuked for "looking at one another," a descriptive expression for the helpless frustration which they must have felt. Being a practical man, Jacob faced the situation realistically. Sitting and bemoaning their fate was certainly no solution. So he called his boys together and sent them on an errand to Egypt to buy grain.

Only Benjamin was kept at home. He was the youngest son and the only surviving descendant of Rachel (Jacob had accepted as a fact that Joseph was dead). Keeping Benjamin at home was a precautionary measure to avoid the possibility of losing the last vestige of hope for the promised kingdom. Who could know but that the sons might be ambushed and murdered for the food which they would have in their possession when returning from Egypt?

Arriving in the sands of Egypt, the Hebrews took their place in the long line of travelers from all over the old world who had come to buy grain. When at last they stood before Joseph, who was robed in his royal garments, they did not recognize him. Concealing his immediate recognition of the brothers who bowed before him, the governor of Egypt accused them of being spies who had come to look at the naked fields.

134

In an effort to prove their honest intent, the brothers insisted that there were 12 of them, all sons of the same father. In addition they explained that one brother was with the father in Canaan and another was "no more," a vague reference to either death or slavery, they knew not which. What strange emotions must have surged through the heart of Joseph at the reference to what the brothers had done to him years before. And looking down at them as they bowed low before him, Joseph remembered the dream he had 20 years earlier, a dream of the brothers' sheaves bowing to his own.

Under pretense of testing their integrity, the governor had the 10 brothers placed in prison for three days, during which time they were to decide which one of them would return to Canaan while the others remained in prison as surety (42:16). Joseph relented, however, and retained only one brother while the other nine returned home to bring Benjamin. Only if they could produce the "brother at home" whom they had mentioned would Joseph believe they were honest!

Simeon was elected to remain, as the brothers flaggelated themselves for what they had done to Joseph. They were in full agreement that what was now happening was judgment upon them for what they did a score of years before.

Not knowing of Joseph's ability to speak their language (an interpreter was present to disguise the fact), the brothers were completely unaware that their condemnation of themselves was understood by this prince. Hearing what they were saying, however, Joseph "turned away from them and wept."

Provisions for the trip were loaded on the pack animals which they had brought. Several bags of grain, which the Hebrews had purchased, were also included. Only after the nine brothers had gotten far down the desert pass did they discover that their money had been stuffed into the bag along with the grain. Trembling with fear, they cried, "What has God done to us?" Their consciences were alive to their evil, and all the evidence indicated that the Lord Himself was against them. They figured that when the Egyptian governor discovered that the suspected spies had stolen the grain, there would be no chance for leniency. They would all be killed. Telling their story to Jacob upon their arrival at home, they opened all the sacks and each one revealed the fearful truth that *every* man had brought back his grain without paying for it.

Heartbroken, Jacob bewailed the death of Joseph, the certain execution of Simeon who had been left for security, and now the obvious possibility that Benjamin and the other nine would be killed if they returned. But if they did not, the whole family would die of starvation. Reuben offered the lives of his own sons as surety for the return of Benjamin from Egypt, but the aging patriarch could not bring himself to enter into a contract which could cost him his grandsons as well as his son. The death of Benjamin would cast his father into Sheol (the second mention of the abode of the dead).

In due time, however, the food ran out, and Judah offered to take full blame if anything happened to the younger brother. There was no time to waste lest the whole clan should die. Forcefully, it was argued that two trips could have been made already if Jacob had not lingered.

With fearful anticipation as to what might happen, Jacob gave his consent, and Benjamin prepared to leave with the other nine. From all appearances, they were taking more into Egypt than they would be bringing out—gum, myrrh, balm, honey, nuts, and almonds. Besides all this, Jacob sent double-payment so as to correct what had happened in the strange turn of events which placed their payment in their bags. With a note of fatalism in his voice, the anxious father raised his hands and forlornly said, "If I am bereaved of my children, I am bereaved" (43:14). But there was also a bit of hope—the only hope—"may God Almighty grant you mercy."

The Joys of a Fraternal Feast (43:16-34)
The sight of young Benjamin was enough to rejoice the heart of the governor, who was standing with his fraternal family while desperately struggling to keep from breaking down. Servants were sent to prepare a feast that Joseph and his brothers might eat together. The men were even escorted to the governor's private quarters, where they went to pieces emotionally. There was little question left as to what was about to happen. Joseph was going to handle them personally for having taken the money. They would be slaves and, what was worst of all, Jacob would die far away with a broken spirit.

In desperation they tried to explain their predicament in regard to the money in the bags of grain. The steward with whom they sought to reason did not rebuke them at all. On the contrary, he assured them that there was no reason for fear since payment had been received. His interpretation of what had happened was that the God of Jacob had miraculously restored their money to them. Soon Simeon joined his brothers where they washed up for the meal and prepared to present their father's gift to the governor.

When the fruits and nuts from his homeland were given to Joseph, he bravely covered up his feelings by inquiring about the health of their father. Assured that he was alive and well, Joseph turned toward Benjamin, asking whether he were the younger son of whom he had heard previously. Quickly the disguised brother pronounced a blessing upon the lad and left the room that he might weep in secret. All the memories of his past, the cherished visions of his dead mother, and the tender scenes from his childhood flooded his mind. He could no longer control himself.

When finally the meal was served, the Egyptians ate at one table, the Hebrews at another, and Joseph at a table by himself. Reuben, the eldest, and Benjamin, the youngest, sat directly across from Joseph and were served from the royal table itself. And for the lad there was a portion five times as large as all the others.

A Plot to Keep Benjamin in Egypt (44:1-34)

As the brothers, gladdened by their success, prepared to depart from Egypt, Joseph instructed his steward to load the grain bags and place each man's money in them again. In Benjamin's bag there was placed the silver cup which belonged to Joseph himself. Soon the party was on its way, only to be stopped by the governor's officer and charged with stealing Joseph's treasured cup. To do such a thing would have been punishable by death since one of the most dastardly deeds of the east was to do one an injustice after having eaten with him. Innocent of the whole plot, the brothers denied any guilt. They were so sure that they agreed to be searched and to have the guilty brother put to death. The sacks were emptied, and the cup was found in Benjamin's grain bag. At their wit's end, the brothers returned to Joseph, their clothing rent, to try to explain the whole thing and to seek an explanation for themselves.

Joseph referred to the silver cup as his divining instrument. Ancients used such cups to read divine guidance. The appearance of the liquid poured into the cup gave enlightenment in difficult times. While the use of such cups sounds like pure superstition to us, apparently God allowed the employment of visible instruments to assist His people in this ancient time of beginnings.

Finding no way to clear themselves, Judah spoke for all the brothers in admitting that Jehovah had found out their guilt (the selling of Joseph, not the stealing of the cup), and they were prepared to be slaves. Being at least "a fair Egyptian," Joseph refused to keep any of the men in custody except the thief himself. That was Benjamin! Nothing worse could have befallen the sons of Jacob than for the youngest son to be taken from their old father. They knew it would utterly crush him.

The scene in Joseph's house which followed is one of the most moving in the entire Bible. Judah, who had been responsible for selling Joseph into slavery at the hands of the passing Midianites, now took the initiative in saving Benjamin from a similar fate. Something had happened in the passing years which changed Judah's hard heart.

The entire story, from the first time the Hebrew brothers saw the Egyptian governor, was recounted by Judah in the presence of his unrecognized brother. In each step he made it clear how perfectly they had sought to carry out the Egyptian's orders. Alas, everything had gone wrong. And if they returned home without Benjamin, their father would die. There was no doubt. Therefore, Judah implored Joseph to let him take the young lad's place and remain as the governor's slave. How utterly beautiful! Perhaps, in this manner, Judah thought that he could offset some of the heartache which he had brought to his family. And he may have surmised that this was also his only chance to compensate before God for what he had done so long ago.

Could it be that Joseph was putting the sons of Jacob through these severe tests to see whether they had made any changes in their evil attitudes? It would have seemed only natural if they had some of the same envious feelings toward Benjamin as they had entertained toward young Joseph, the dreamer. In both cases, the boys were the father's favorite sons. If Judah wanted the birthright, he might still have a problem as long as Benjamin, the only surviving son of Jacob's favorite wife, Rachel, was around. Joseph knew that if the brothers left Benjamin in Egypt as a slave, they would be doing precisely the same thing they had earlier done to him—and for the same evil end. But they passed the test with flying colors. It was clear that their attitudes were changed and that they were entitled to a place in the family's preservation.

The Reappearance of a Lost Brother (45:1—46:34)
The reunion (45:1-28)

At last the time had come. No longer able to control his emotions, the governor cleared his house of all his servants and officers. Then, with a burst of pent-up emotion, Joseph wept, the tears gushing like fountains from his eyes and his body shaking under the fierce impact of his brokenness. His crying was so loud that the people outside heard it, and even those in the house of Pharaoh himself were startled by the sound of weeping.

When Joseph finally revealed his identity and asked about his old father, the brothers were so stunned that they were unable to speak. Calling them to come closer, Joseph convinced them that he was the one whom they had sold into slavery 22 years prior to that time (the famine had now completed two years). Furthermore, he explained to them that the famine would continue for five more years. At once he allayed their fears and chided them for being angry with themselves for what they had done to him.

No one has ever been more fully convinced of the sovereign plan and power of God than was Joseph. What his brothers had done seemed evil at the time, but even their deed of fraternal treachery had been used by the Lord to preserve His people in a time of famine. If they had not sold Joseph, he would never have become governor in control of the granaries of Egypt. And without that one step in the divine design, the covenant itself would have been lost on an extinct family. But once the Lord begins, He always finishes. The kingdom which was promised to the Hebrews was yet to be given to them. Joseph knew this and, even after 20 years in a pagan land where he was married to a pagan woman, he never lost faith in the covenant given to his ancestors. Through Joseph in Egypt, God was preserving "a *remnant* on earth." This is the first mention of a remnant, which played so large a role in succeeding years as the Lord led His people through prosperity and adversity.

Embracing one another, Joseph and Benjamin wept for joy. With the impatience of one away from home so long, Joseph instructed his brothers to go back to Canaan and bring their father and all his possessions to dwell in Egypt until the famine was over. When Pharaoh heard of what was taking place, he sanctioned the plan and promised the best, most fertile lands in Egypt to Joseph's family. The land of Goshen was to be theirs—the Egyptian delta in the northeastern part of the country where grazing was excellent. In addition all the brothers were loaded with "festal garments" and Benjamin was given an entire wardrobe! Gifts of lavish value were sent to Jacob along with wagons and horses to transport the family back to Egypt.

As the caravan departed, Joseph cautioned them not to quarrel (probably remembering their old natures) but to return as quickly as possible with Jacob. The understatement of the Genesis account is "when he saw the wagons which Joseph had sent to carry him, the spirit of Jacob their father revived" (45:27). That seems not to say nearly enough. We can hardly imagine how Jacob felt in that moment.

The people who came (46:1-34)

Jacob came from Hebron with his descendants and wealth. At Beersheba, the exit from the land of Canaan, he stopped to offer sacrifices, recalling that the Lord had specifically told Isaac in a time of famine not to go down into Egypt (Gen. 26:1-6). When Abraham had traveled into the land of the Nile, he experienced only trouble (Gen. 12:10-20), and came near to upsetting the Lord's plans for a great nation. It was extremely important that Jacob know whether the ban on such migration had been lifted.

In the vision which came that night, the Lord made it clear that it was now within the divine plan for the family to live in Egypt, but only temporarily. The promise was that the Hebrews would one day be brought out of the pagan land and restored to their home in Canaan. God even told Jacob that He would make him into a great nation while away from home. The reference to Joseph's hand closing his eyes (46:4) was most likely a comforting assurance that Jacob's favorite son, whom the father had thought dead, would be with him at his death to tenderly shut his eyelids.

The lengthy roster of names which follows in this chapter includes all the descendants of Jacob who were living at that time and who went with him into Egypt. His sons, grandsons, daughters, granddaughters, and any other offspring attributed to Jacob are named, the total being 70 persons. The number 70 was probably a round number and not intended as an exact figure.

Judah was sent ahead of the rest of the family to meet Joseph in Goshen. When Jacob finally arrived, his son who "was dead and is alive again" (Luke 15:24) fell on his neck and wept. The embrace was a long and tender one, followed by Jacob's relaxed confidence that, having seen his boy alive, he was ready now to depart in peace.

Joseph was a man of great strategy and discretion. Knowing that the Egyptians considered shepherds the lowest stratum of human life (the Egyptians were agriculturists and had often been attacked by roving shepherd tribes), Joseph suggested that Pharaoh be told of the long line of shepherds which formed the ancestry of Jacob's sons. Thus they would be assigned to the delta in Goshen, an area where the Egyptians did little growing (most of the agriculture was carried on farther south in the canal lands). Actually it was the best of all Egypt's pasture lands!

God's sovereignty is magnified so clearly in the life of Joseph and in the development of the other children of Israel. How important and exciting to be in on God's plans today through personal faith in Jesus Christ. In that environment of trust, we rest on the New Testament counterpart of Joseph's feelings expressed in Genesis 50:20: "As for you [the brothers], you meant evil against me, but God meant it for good" (NASB). Our assurance is: "And we know that God causes all things to work together for good to those who love God, to those who are called according to His purpose" (Rom. 8:28, NASB).

12
ISRAEL AWAY FROM HOME

Genesis 47:1—49:32

The Family Dwells in Goshen (47:1-12)

As Joseph had anticipated, Pharaoh allowed the Hebrews to settle in Goshen and asked that Joseph appoint the best shepherds among them to tend the royal cattle. In an interview between Pharaoh and Jacob, the king inquired as to Jacob's age—130 years. Jacob spoke of his days as *few* compared to his patriarchal ancestors' and admitted that they had been *evil*, a recall of his years of deception and selfishness. Then Jacob blessed the Egyptian king and went to live among his own people in the land of Goshen (called "the land of Rameses," a later title). They were to remain there for 430 years until one named *Moses* should arise to set them free.

The Manner of Joseph's Rule (47:13-31)

Eventually, as we would suspect, people spent all their money buying food from Joseph. The treasury of Egypt grew fat. When the people complained that they had no more money, Joseph asked that they buy grain in exchange for their cattle. And when the cattle were gone, the people offered to sell themselves into slavery for food. "So Joseph bought all the land of Egypt for Pharaoh" (except that which had been dedicated for holy purposes to the priests) and made slaves of all the people. The priests were cared for personally by the king, who provided their needs in return for their divine blessing and guidance. In exchange for the titles to their land and the deeds to their souls, Joseph gave seed to the people to plant the fields. One-fifth of the harvest would belong to Pharaoh and the rest of the products to the people themselves.

While it may appear to us that such an arrangement was not in keeping with the gentle nature of Joseph, it must be acknowledged that times of famine required strict supervision. The slavery which the Hebrew governor was responsible for was literally an act of gracious kindness. Only with governmental administration such as he proposed could the people survive. Obviously the enslavement of the people under Joseph was a humanitarian program for the people's good in a time of international emergency. The slavery which *later* came to the Hebrews under a different Pharaoh was a bitter and galling thing which dehumanized people. But for the Egyptians to be given 80 percent of what they produced was in line with the policy of more humane nations of today's world.

For 17 years Jacob lived in the land of Goshen. These were delightful times for him as he watched his family multiply and his flocks increase. God was blessing him as He had promised. The fact that the Hebrews did not make their living by tilling the soil plus the fact that Pharaoh pledged his faithfulness to Joseph's family may mean that they were exempt from the legalized slavery voluntarily assumed by the Egyptians. By the time of the famine's end, especially by the time of Jacob's death, the descendants of Abraham were growing wealthy and powerful.

Notwithstanding his love for the Egyptian delta, Jacob did not want to be buried in Pharaoh's land. The desire was so strong that Joseph was called and made to promise that he would return with his father's remains to the Promised Land. The same kind of oath was demanded of him as Abraham had demanded of his old servant (Gen. 24:1-9). Placing Joseph's hand under Jacob's thigh may have been a threat of impotence in the event the vow was not performed. The old patriarch, now 147 years old, forced Joseph to swear that he would bury him with Abraham and Isaac.

A Hebrew Blessing Overrules Egyptian Power (48:1-22)
News was brought to Joseph that his father had grown weaker and was rapidly approaching death. Fearing that this might be the last time he would see Jacob alive, he took with him his two sons, Manasseh and Ephraim, both born in Egypt. The sickly

father mustered all his remaining strength and sat up in bed to bless Joseph. The blessing began with a recapitulation of the covenant which came first to Abraham, then to Isaac, and finally to Jacob. It was the same covenant in each case, always affirming unconditionally for the Hebrews productivity, progeny, power, and a kingdom which would never end. Jacob remembered it in detail from the first time he had heard it for himself directly from the Eternal at Bethel, when he was running from Esau.

The blessing was different, however, than even Joseph may have anticipated. Jacob reasoned with paternal authority that the two sons born to Joseph in Egypt were to be adopted as the grandfather's own sons. They would share equally with Reuben and the rest of the sons of Jacob. Reuben and Simeon are mentioned by name since they were the first and second sons born to the aged patriarch. By comparing Manasseh and Ephraim to them he was giving them equal status with the oldest of his children. Future children born to Joseph or to his sons would be the sons of Joseph, but these two were now to become legally the sons of Jacob. In some mysterious, symbolic way, the sons of Joseph would complete the dreams which Jacob had for more children by Rachel, who had died in giving birth to her second son. Reuben and Simeon, having forfeited the birthright by their wickedness, would be replaced by or supplemented with Manasseh and Ephraim.

Israel's (Jacob's) eyes were dim with age and he had not noticed the two grandsons, about whom he had been talking, standing in the shadows of his room. When he became aware of their presence he asked who they were and, hearing that they were Joseph's sons, he called them to the bedside that he might adopt and bless them (48:9). When Joseph later took his two sons from the knees of Jacob, we are to understand that being there was a symbol of legitimate sonship or adoption (48:12). Concubines' children were born across the knees of the favored wife as a symbol of acceptance into the family. The imagery is the same in either case.

Joseph carefully placed his two sons so that each would receive the proper blessing. The older, Manasseh, was positioned at Israel's right hand, and the younger, Ephraim, at his left. The "right hand blessing" was for the firstborn. When the blessing was given, Joseph sought to correct what he thought to be a mistake. The old man had crossed his arms in a manner which placed his right hand upon the head of the younger son. But Israel would have it no other way. That which he had done was deliberate.

We see here a repetition. The older Esau was replaced by the younger Jacob when Isaac gave his final blessing. Indelibly etched on Jacob's memory, that experience may have influenced Israel to repeat the old performance. In the instance before us, however, there was no deceit. Israel knew that Manasseh would become a great nation but Ephraim would become still greater. In light of the fulfillment of the dying man's prophecy, it would be incredible for anyone to fail to see the hand of Almighty God in Israel's decision to choose Ephraim over Manasseh.

Israel promised that the time would come when Joseph's descendants would be brought back to Canaan by the hand of God. The blessing pronounced on Joseph and Ephraim gave the "mountain slope," which had been seized from the Amorites (Canaanites) by force, to the tribe of Ephraim (48:22, AMP). "Mountain slope" is the same word as is used for the city of *Shechem*. The most prominent mount in the area was Mount Gerizim, probably the "mountain slope" referred to in the promise. The statement about his having taken Shechem "with my sword and my bow" must be a reference to Simeon and Levi's massacre of the circumcised men who dwelt there (Gen. 34). Though the sons had been punished for what they had done, Israel may have come to think of that vanquished city as his own. It is a fact that the area around Shechem and Mount Gerizim became the home of the people of Ephraim.

Blessings For All in the House (49:1-32)
Observations on his sons (49:1-28)
Beginning with the firstborn, Israel offered words of prediction and advice to each of his sons. Reuben, who had been guilty of adultery with Bilhah (Gen. 35:22; 1 Chron. 5:1), could not be trusted by a dying father to have *preeminence* over the family. He had been preeminent "in pride and power" and, due to his abuse of that position, was disqualified from the birthright. Reuben was far too *unstable* for such responsibility. The tribe of Reuben settled in the southern half of what had been known as Sihon, in trans-Jordon at the northeast end of the Dead Sea. During the ninth century before Christ, the Moabites (neighbors to the south)

took over the territory of Reuben and the tribe disappeared from history.

Simeon and Levi were given a joint blessing since they seem to have been extremely close in their relationship with each other and due to their massacre of the people of Shechem (Gen. 34:25-31). Israel called them "a pair" (two of a kind) and rejected them as being of a wanton and malicious nature which he could not condone. For their "anger, wantonness, wrath, and cruelty" they lost their inheritance. They were to be *divided* and *scattered* among the other tribes with no lasting territory of their own. Simeon was assigned to dwell "within the inheritance of the children of Judah" (Josh. 19:1-9; 1 Chron. 4:28-33). By the time of the second census (Num. 26:14), the people of Simeon had dwindled to become the lowest of the tribes. Levi was left no territory at all but destined to live among all the tribes. In time the descendants of Levi became the priests (Levites) who permeated like leaven the life and culture of the entire kingdom. We wonder at the ways of God which are "past finding out" (Rom. 11:33).

Judah was promised the sceptre of leadership. Being the fourth-born after Reuben, Simeon, and Levi (who had been denied the birthright), he was the rightful contender for the place of preeminence. His strength was praised and his brothers were destined to respect his position. At both the first and second census takings in the new land, the tribe of Judah was the largest in population. Thus he "prevailed above his brethren" (1 Chron. 5:2). Israel's prophecy included a choice territory which would be rich with vineyards and prosperity. When all the allotments were made, a full third of the land west of the Jordan was allocated to the people of Judah.

The most important prediction relating to this son regards his place in the genealogy of Christ. Judah was to retain the sceptre of leadership "until He comes to whom it belongs." The Hebrew word here which sets forth the Messianic hope is *Shiloh,* both the name of a place and a person (49:10). Hebrew and Christian scholars are agreed that Israel is here prophesying the coming of the Messiah. When this One came, He would take the sceptre from Judah and reign over *all* the peoples. The Messiah came in Jesus Christ, an offspring of the tribe of Judah, who will conquer all the kingdoms of man as "the Lion of the tribe of Judah" (Rev. 5:5). Though Christ was rejected by the Jews when He came the first time, He will come again to set up His kingdom and reign as Prince of Peace forever!

Zebulun was predicted to "dwell at the seashore" (49:13) and be "a haven for ships." His territory was to be midway between the Mediterranean Sea and the Sea of Galilee. Though Zebulun did not actually touch the shore of the Galilean Sea in the time of the Judges, it may have done so later. Issachar is closely identified in the patriarchal blessing and did touch the Sea at its southwest corner. In a sense Zebulun had complete access to the Sea since Issachar was a thoroughfare. It is known that Zebulun was a strong commercial people using the seas for their trade. The reference to Sidon was probably a designation of the general Phoenician area of which Sidon was a chief city. The west flank of the highlands of the Sea of Galilee did border Phoenician territory in the Plain of Accho, the area settled by Zebulun.

Issachar was situated at the southwest end of the Sea of Galilee and ranked third in population size at the time of the second census (Num. 26:25). The blessing refers to Issachar's strength but is not very complimentary. The tribe is seen following the path of least resistance and eventually allowing marauders to settle in the rich territory—outsiders to whom Issachar actually paid tribute!

The tribe of Dan was associated with judging (a prophecy fulfilled in Samson, the Danite judge). Furthermore, the tribe is said to be like a serpent, subtle and treacherous. This may be a reference to the sneak attack on the city of Laish in the far north which the people of Dan rebuilt, naming it after their ancestor. Dan, the city so named, formed the northern extreme geographically of the land of promise, even as Beersheba served as the southern property-marker. The tribe itself was given territory over 100 miles southwest of the conquered city. It bordered the Mediterranean Sea, between Judah and Ephraim, and was the smallest land portion given to any tribe. Israel's cry, at the end of Dan's blessing—"I wait for thy salvation, O Lord" (49:18, AMP)—may have been an outburst of remorse over his own treacherous ways and a deep distress that Dan would make the same error in depending on his own ingenuity in achieving supremacy.

Gad shared, in the old land territory of Sihon, with Reuben on the east side of Jordan, about halfway between the northern and southern boundaries of Canaan. The land was high, with excellent grazing for flocks and herds. Since Gad had an abundance of cattle, the area was ideal for the occupation of its chief men. But the land was open to attacks from the eastern desert, especially from the Ammonites. However, Gad's ability to defend himself was equal to the pressure which was predicted to come from outside. Eventually, in spite of their defenses, the people of Gad were captured by Tiglath-pileser and deported to Assyria (2 Kings 15:29, 1 Chron: 5:26).

Asher was situated on the extreme northern shore of the Mediterranean Sea, an extremely rich and fertile area, which accounts for the "rich food" and "royal dainties." This affluent living may have contributed to the sterility of the tribe which had become so insignificant as not to be included in the Davidic list of chief rulers. Perhaps dwelling in proximity with the pagan Phoenicians added weight to their degeneration as well.

The tribe of Naphtali was appointed land adjacent to Asher and to its east. He was predicted to be agile and vocal. Subject to continuous attacks by outside forces, the tribe was finally the first to be captured by Assyria under Tiglath-pileser in the eighth century before Christ.

There seems to be no end to the good things predicted for Joseph, the slave-dreamer who saved the whole family from death. He was destined to be fruitful and invulnerable to the tribal attacks from pagan peoples who lived about him. His land area, divided between Ephraim (central on the west of Jordan) and Manasseh (both east and west of Jordan and north of Ephraim), comprised nearly one-half of the land of Canaan. Though Manasseh had the larger land area and the most advanced material prosperity, Ephraim was politically stronger. Ephraim, because of the unwise leadership of Rehoboam after the death of Solomon, seceded from the kingdom, forming the 10 tribes of the north. Of this kingdom, Ephraim was the prime support. The tribe went into captivity in 721 B.C.

The wolfish character of Benjamin comes through again and again in his descendants: Ehud (Jud. 3), Gibeah (Jud. 20), and the entire career of Saul. This latter name brings to mind at once that it was the tribe of Benjamin who produced the first king of Israel. The small territory given to Benjamin was northwest of the Dead Sea, nestled between Judah and Ephraim with Dan bordering its western frontier. Eventually, in the hostilities which developed after the time of Saul, Benjamin came increasingly to be associated with Judah until the little wolf-like tribe practically lost its identity.

The blessings concluded with a charge (49:29-32)

With his strength now exhausted from the ordeal of blessing 12 sons and prophesying their futures, Israel charged his sons not to fail in carrying out his wishes about being buried in Canaan. Careful specifics are given by which none of the sons could be confused as to the precise cave of the patriarchs at Hebron. Jacob even retraced the history of the purchase of the area in which the cave was located and reminded his family of boys that five of his loved ones had already been buried there. He mentioned the burial of Leah (whose death has not been referred to until now) at Hebron and apparently desired to be buried beside her. This strikes us as being a bit strange since Rachel was his favorite wife. But Rachel died while journeying back to Canaan from the house of Laban and was buried beside the roadway. Leah probably died much later under less pressured conditions. Thus Jacob was able to bury his older wife at Hebron. Burial for himself with the fathers of the clan took precedence over interment beside a beloved wife.

It was a touching scene—an old man making arrangements for his death and dictating to his grieving sons exactly how and where his funeral should be conducted. He had tasted many flavors of life, and suffered extensively over some of the bitter ones. But Jacob-Israel knew God, and was a vital part in His story.

13
EX POST
FACTO

Genesis 49:33—50:26

With the blessings on his sons completed and the instructions about his death ended, Israel did not wait long for death. The description of the last moment in the life of this son of Isaac seems almost melodramatic at first. But people often die as quickly and easily as he when their last preparation has been made. Drawing his feet up in his bed and breathing his last, Jacob moved into a more spacious and joyous place than even his beloved Canaan promised to be. All the deep fountains of grief burst forth from Joseph's soul as he fell upon his father's face and wept.

Embalming procedures in Egypt were meticulous. Most of the interior of the deceased man's head and abdomen was removed by the physicians. The shell of the body was then carefully treated for preservation. Forty days were spent in embalming Jacob, and the Egyptians wept and wailed over him 70 days, almost as long as the official mourning period for a king himself. When the days for mourning were over, Joseph requested leave of Pharaoh to go to Canaan to bury his father. Not only was permission given, but great numbers of the leading men of state, military officers, and personal servants formed an entourage to escort the body to its grave. "It was a very great company" (50:9).

Somewhere in Canaan at a place called *Atad,* the party stopped and observed seven days of mourning for Jacob. The Canaanites observed the loud weeping of the Egyptians and were impressed by the importance of the occasion. It may be that the funeral party stopped for the purpose of allowing Jacob's Canaanite friends to pay their last respects to the great man who had lived among them. The place was named, as was customary for the ancients, in deference to the event which transpired there: *Abel-mizraim* (mourning of Egypt).

After seven days at Atad, the entouraged moved on to Hebron and, with proper ceremonies, laid the body of the third patriarch to rest in the cave of Machpelah.

Abraham, Isaac, Jacob-Israel—the great triad of Hebrew fathers —were now dead, and the times of slavery were soon to begin.

Now that Israel was gone, the sons feared that Joseph might treat them harshly for what they had done to him at Dothan. A messenger, perhaps Judah or Benjamin, was sent to the governor with a report that Jacob had asked for reconciliation between Joseph and his 11 brothers. It is quite probable that the dying father not only wanted Joseph to forgive, but that he also wanted the others to *ask* forgiveness. No mention has been made before about such a request on the part of the sons who had sold Joseph into slavery. When the report of Jacob's wishes was made known to Joseph, he wept in love for his brethren, pointing out that judgment must come from God, not from one's brother. Then, with great insight, the wronged brother expressed one of history's finest truths: "As for you, you meant evil against me; but God meant it for good" (50:20, NASB). With this fact before them, he reassured his brothers of his good will and eternal love.

At the age of 110 years Joseph died. He was embalmed and buried in Egypt by the people of two countries—both of which loved him and deeply respected his wisdom. Before his death he saw his son's grandchildren. The children of Manasseh's son were born upon his knee, a symbol of legitimate sonship in the family.

A promise similar to that which Jacob had given to Joseph was in turn given by the latter to his brothers. The day would come when God would bring the people of Abraham, Isaac, and Jacob out of Egypt and make them a great kingdom—a kingdom which would have no end. The sons of Israel were made to promise that, when that time came, they would disinter Joseph's bones and carry them into the land of promise. How great was Joseph's faith in God! He was sure that God would do what He had promised. So like Abraham, Isaac, and Jacob before him, Joseph would rest at last in Canaan.

The Kingdom of Israel

Here ends the epic of Genesis. And here begins the kingdom of Israel. The next 400 years were to be times of hardship, harder than anything the prospering sons of Israel could imagine. Had Abraham been still alive he would have known what to expect, for many years before he had been warned.* In a strange appearance of the lord in smoke and fire, Abraham had been told that four centuries of slavery in a strange land were in the nation's future (Gen. 15:13-14). Soon a new Pharaoh was to come to the throne in Egypt, a king who did not honor Joseph's memory (Ex. 1:8) or respect his father's descendants. The Hebrews would be subjected to forced labor and the most beastly kind of slavery. As had been true at each preceding moment of human hopelessness, so it was to be again—the God of Israel would prepare a solution to the impossible situation. Trained in the royal courts by divine providence, young Moses would at last contest the powers of Pharaoh and lead the people of Abraham to freedom.

Following the death of Moses, the children of the Exodus would be led in the conquest of Canaan under the capable military strategist, Joshua. Once the land was in control of the Hebrews (and Joshua was dead), judges would be appointed to handle matters of discontent. It would be a bloody, barbarous age of anarchy. So the people would demand a king. The first one, Saul, would be succeeded by David and then his son, Solomon. After Solomon, the nation would break apart into a northern and southern kingdom. Most of the kings after Solomon, in both kingdoms, would be wicked. The people would descend into idolatry like the Canaanites, either initiating degenerating moral lapse or giving impetus to already existing apostasy.

By the eighth century, the prophets would be crying out against the neglect of true worship and the prevalence of social injustice. In the last quarter of that century the northern kingdom would be seized and conquered by the Assyrians from the north. Then less than 150 years later the powerful Babylonians would sack Judah (the southern kingdom) and carry the Jews into captivity.

During the exile in Babylonia, which would last 70 years, Ezekiel and Daniel would prophesy strange and wonderful things

---

* For a panoramic view and full account of the entire history of Israel from Abraham until the finalization of the divine kingdom, read the author's *Population, Pollution, and Prophecy* (Fleming H. Revell, Old Tappan, N.J.).

to the despairing captives. They would talk about the kingdom which God had promised to Abraham, a dream which had been all but forgotten by the Jews far from home. Both prophets would foresee the people of the covenant in control of Canaan again, led by the heir to David's throne, the Messianic Deliverer.

Inspired by this talk about the glories of the future there would be a stirring among the people and rumors of returning to their native land. With the permission of Cyrus, a motley throng of Jews would return to rebuild the Temple in Jerusalem in the latter half of the sixth century. By the middle of the following century Nehemiah would lead a Jewish construction crew in rebuilding the walls of the city. For the next 500 years numerous puppet kings would sit on David's throne and pretend to reign, the fires of hope reduced to smoldering embers by the time of Jesus of Nazareth. Some would feel the sparks fly upward at the suggestion that this carpenter's Son might redeem Israel from the oppressing hand of her latest captor. Alas, He would finally be crucified (and resurrected!—but many would not believe that), and the last vestige of the Temple would be swept away in the revolt of the Jews against Rome in A.D. 70. But God would not even then be through with Israel.

All over the world the sons of Abraham would be scattered. The dispersion would be universal. Everywhere the Hebrew people would prosper and multiply. And everywhere they would be persecuted. Nations and people who mistreated the Jews would suffer for it. Those who befriended them would "bless themselves" even as God promised to Abraham long ago.

Still the prophetic clock would tick away the moments on the Lord's eternal timetable. By the 20th century, practically all the prophecies would be fulfilled. For the first time since the days of Titus, the Jews would go back home, just as Ezekiel and Daniel predicted. The restored nation of Israel would thrive in the land of promise. Jerusalem would belong to the Jews and the desert would blossom as the rose. Even the Hebrew language would be reborn for the people in the streets of Jerusalem. One thing would remain—the return of the Lord Jesus Christ to sit on David's throne.

When Abram was 99 years old the Lord appeared to Abram and said to him, "I am God Almighty; walk before Me and be blameless. And I will establish My covenant between Me and you, and I will multiply you exceedingly." And Abram fell on his face; and God talked with him, saying, "As for Me, behold, My covenant is with you and you shall be the father of a multitude of nations. No longer shall your name be called Abram, but your name shall be Abraham; for I will make you the father of a multitude of nations. I will make you exceedingly fruitful; and I will make nations of you, and kings shall come forth from you. And I will establish My covenant between Me and you and your descendants after you throughout their generations for an *everlasting covenant,* to be God to you and to your descendants after you. And I will give to you, and to your descendants after you, the land of your sojournings, all the land of Canaan, for an *everlasting possession;* and I will be their God" (Gen. 17:1-8, NASB).

So be it! For the kingdom of God shall know no end. And toward its perfect coming all creation moves. Amen, and amen!

Inspirational Books
for your Enjoyment

☐ **KNOW WHY YOU BELIEVE** by Paul E. Little, of Trinity Evangelical Divinity School. Discusses the rationality of Christianity, and helps believers in giving a reason for their faith. Textbook **6-2022—$1.75**/Leader's Guide **6-2929—95¢**

☐ **KNOW WHAT YOU BELIEVE** by Paul E. Little. Discusses the validity of the evangelical position on vital doctrines of the Christian Church. Textbook **6-2024—$1.75** Leader's Guide **6-2933—95¢**

☐ **YOU CAN BE TRANSFORMED** by Larry Richards. A practical and relevant study of the book of Luke, God's Gospel of New Life. Textbook **6-2236—$1.75**/Leader's Guide **6-2907—95¢**

☐ **THE ACTS—THEN AND NOW** by Henry Jacobsen. A practical and enriching study of the New Testament Book of Acts. Textbook **6-2239—$1.95**/Leader's Guide **6-2906—$1.25**

☐ **THE WAR WE CAN'T LOSE** by Henry Jacobsen. A devotional and encouraging study of the Book of the Revelation. Textbook **6-2047—$1.25**/Leader's Guide **6-2936—95¢**

☐ **THE BIBLE AND TOMORROW'S NEWS** by Dr. Charles C. Ryrie, of Dallas Theological Seminary. Discusses, from a dispensational and premillenarian viewpoint, what the Bible says about the times in which we live and the end of the age. Textbook **6-2017—$1.75**/Leader's Guide **6-2932—95¢**

☐ **FACING TODAY'S PROBLEMS** A symposium on today's outstanding issues, treated from an evangelical viewpoint, by authorities in their respective fields. Textbook **6-2025—$1.50**/Leader's Guide **6-2934—95¢**

**Buy these titles at your local Christian bookstore
or order from Scripture Press.**

Scripture Press Publications, Inc.
Wheaton, Illinois 60187

Please send me the books checked above. I am enclosing
$_____ plus 15¢ per book for postage and handling.
(Enclose check or money order—no currency or C.O.D.s.)

Name_____

Address_____

City_____State_____Zip_____

Inspirational Books for your Enjoyment

☐ **THE FAMILY THAT MAKES IT** A biblical-approach symposium on the Christian home. Down-to-earth help on keeping a family together in a day when evil forces tear it apart. Textbook **6-2045—$1.75**/Leader's Guide **6-2935—95¢**

☐ **THE FRAGRANCE OF BEAUTY** by Joyce Landorf. Scripturally based study of wrong attitudes that can mar a woman's beauty—and help for correcting them. Textbook **6-2231—$1.25**/Leader's Guide **6-2912—95¢**

☐ **ME BE LIKE JESUS?** by Leslie B. Flynn. Discusses the character of the Lord Jesus Christ as examples for a Christian to develop. Textbook **6-2234—$1.75**/Leader's Guide **6-2904—95¢**

☐ **THE SPIRIT WORLD** A study of the occult by McCandlish Phillips, a Christian newsman. Shows the reader he can triumph over the power of Satan by turning to God and His superior forces. Textbook **6-2048—$1.75**/Leader's Guide **6-2900—95¢**

☐ **THE GOOD LIFE** A practical and relevant study of the Epistle of James by Henry Jacobsen, senior editor of Scripture Press All-Bible Adult Sunday School lessons. Textbook **6-2018—$1.75**/Leader's Guide **6-2930—95¢**

☐ **THE STRUGGLE FOR PEACE** by Dr. Henry R. Brandt, Christian psychologist. A fresh and Christian approach to mental health problems. Textbook **6-2023—$1.25**/Leader's Guide **6-2931—95¢**

☐ **BUILDING A CHRISTIAN HOME** by Henry R. Brandt. A practical, biblical, evangelical approach to family living. Textbook **6-2051—$2.00**/Leader's Guide **6-2928—95¢**

Buy these titles at your local Christian bookstore or order from Scripture Press.

Scripture Press Publications, Inc.
Wheaton, Illinois 60187

Please send me the books checked above. I am enclosing $_____ plus 15¢ per book for postage and handling (Enclose check or money order—no currency or C.O.D.s.)

Name_____

Address_____

City_____State_____Zip_____